Hwange

RETREAT *of the* ELEPHANTS

Hwange
RETREAT *of the* ELEPHANTS

Written & Photographed by Nick Greaves

SOUTHERN
BOOK PUBLISHERS

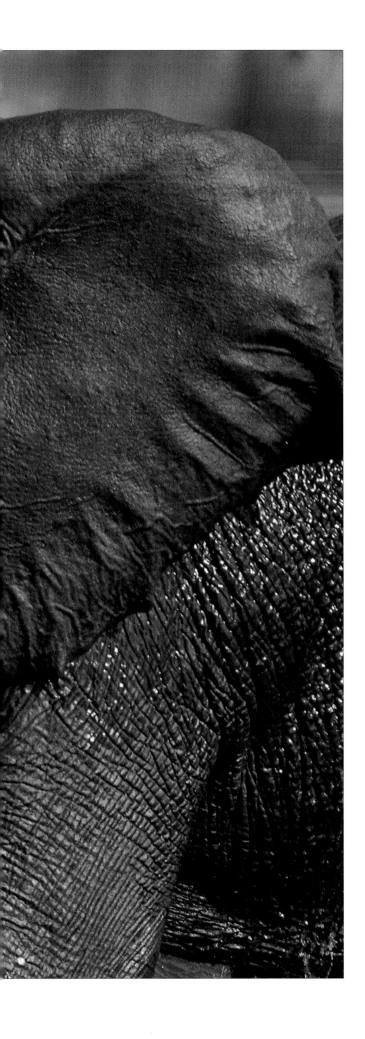

CONTENTS

ISBN 1-86812-665-X

First edition, first impression 1996

Published by
Southern Book Publishers (Pty) Ltd
PO Box 3103,
Halfway House, 1685

Cover design by: Alix Gracie
Cover photograph by: Nick Greaves
Maps by: Alix Gracie
Designed by: Alix Gracie
Set in: Bembo 10.5/13
Reproduction: cmyk prepress,
Cape Town

Printed and bound by:
National Book Printers, Drukkery Street
Goodwood, Western Cape

Author's note

Hwange seems like a big, remote, unspoilt and often inhos-
pitable wilderness to man, but to the elephant, Hwange is
home. Hwange's reputation grows as the best place left in
Africa for viewing large numbers of free-roaming elephants.
This reputation is further enhanced as the elephants become
more accustomed to the presence of humans.

But ivory poaching is a constant threat in Hwange as in all
of Africa and if the ivory trade is ever legalised again the current trickle would turn overnight into a tidal wave of death
and destruction. Southern Africa — with the exception of
Mozambique — escaped the horrors of large-scale, organised ivory poaching during the 1980s, but Zimbabwe was
unable to save the rhino during this era. What chance do we
have of saving the elephants if there is a renewed vicious
onslaught of poaching? As matters stand at present, the
answer would have to be very little at all.

I love elephants and make no apology for it. To spend
hours, days or years in close proximity to wild elephants is
both a joy and a privilege. I hope many others will be able
to enjoy and appreciate such close contact and, above all,
that this opportunity will exist for our children's children.

Only with such intimate contact can we unravel the mysteries of the elephant, its habitat, its co-inhabitants, its
Hwange ...

*'A man cannot spend his life in Africa without acquiring some-
thing pretty close to a great affection for the elephants. These great
herds are, after all, the last symbol of liberty left among us.'*
(Roots of Heaven, *Romain Gary 1958).*

Nick Greaves
1996

Hwange
RETREAT *of the* ELEPHANTS

*'... for a transitory enchanted moment, Man must have held his breath in
the presence of this Continent, compelled into an aesthetic contemplation he neither
understood nor desired, face to face for the last time in history with something
commensurate to his capacity for wonder.'*

F Scott Fitzgerald

Prologue

Although this book is ostensibly about Hwange, its haunting beauty and the facilities and opportunities it offers the visitor, both local and foreign, it is also about the plight and dilemmas faced by some of its inhabitants. Hwange is vast and only a small area is easily accessible to the casual visitor, but even in the more frequented areas one cannot help but feel the magic of the wilderness.

It is ironic that Hwange's main drawcards today are its tracts of unspoilt bush, empty of human interference. The park was originally created purely because the authorities could not put it to any other more 'beneficial' use. The area, mostly expanses of woodland and Kalahari sands that lack surface water for most of the year, was unsuited to agriculture, extensive logging of its indigenous hardwoods or ranching and, as such, could serve no better function than a game reserve. The numbers of most species had not recovered from decades of uncontrolled hunting in the early era of colonial settlement so Hwange could not even be used as a controlled hunting area.

Only with the provision of artificial water supplies, which guaranteed reliable surface water throughout the year, did Hwange's inhabitants manage to form stable and resident breeding populations. Concentrating animals in a fixed area, no matter how large, was inevitably going to lead to a change in the habitat. In essence, this vast wilderness was created by man for the wildlife, but since it is man-made, a dilemma presents itself. Does man stand by and let the animals alter the wilderness until nature finds its own balance — no matter what the consequences — or does he step in and restore the habitat to what he thinks is a natural balance, no matter how unpopular the means may be?

This vexatious question has been debated across Africa for decades and Zimbabwe remains in the forefront of the war of words over elephant culling and ivory trading. Hwange and its elephant are at the heart of this war — and both are in the firing line.

Acknowledgements

I wish to thank the Director of the Department of National Parks and Wildlife Management, Dr Willie Nduku, and the former Deputy Director Dr Rowan Martin for the necessary permissions and clearances to undertake this lengthy project. The assistance of Mrs Anne Moore, former Warden: Tourism was invaluable in obtaining these clearances.

I wish to extend my most grateful thanks to all the National Parks staff based in Hwange, both past and present. These include Ron Thomson, the late Babs Thomson, Rob Murray, Mike Jones, the late Fanuel Nare, Frank and Jasmine Potts, Gavin and Shay Best, Ivan Ncube, Kit Hustler, Andy Searle, Barney O'Hara, Sgt Richard Ndlovu, Mr Dick Shirinyodza, Norman English, Tommy Orford and the many members of staff in the various tourist offices. I would also like to express my gratitude to all the scouts, especially Elias Banda, whose selfless acts of courage, valour and hardship against mounting odds are the greatest hope for the continued future of Zimbabwe's wildlife and wilderness areas.

Also I wish to thank Alan and Scottie Elliott and their staff at Touch The Wild for their kind help over the years, especially Lionel and Brenda Reynolds, Bryn and Perry Jolliffe, Ross Johnson, Raphael Ndlovu, Aubrey Packenham, Mark Edwards and Garth Thompson. Special thanks go to Ron and all the White family, Craig, Carol, Shayne, Libby, and all the kids and especially to the memory of Jean whom we all miss so much, and the staff at Jijima Safari Camp for their fantastic hospitality. Mark Butcher, John Burton, Trevor Lane, Mark McCaul, John Nicholson, Rich and Bookie Peek, Paul Perez, Tish Lee, Greg Rasmussen, and Kathy Rogers: thanks also for the help you all rendered.

Thanks also to Will Travers and all at Elefriends and the Born Free Foundation. Also to Allen Thornton, Dave Currey and Suzy Watts at the EIA. The work done by these people and organisations has been, and continues to be, the saving grace for the elephant.

Without the technical support of Canon Inc of Japan this project would have fallen flat many years ago. I am deeply indebted to Mr T D Nozaki and his technical staff at Canon for their speedy and highly efficient repairs and servicing. Without their help I would have been lost.

Special thanks go to Mr Lloyd Deenik of Eastman Kodak, USA, and Mr Brian Paddy of Zimbabwe Photographic, local agents for Kodak. Without their kind donation of transparency film, Kodachrome 25 and 64 the project would never have gained momentum.

Vital assistance was also given by Wankie Colliery Company and thanks go to Mr George Julyan and Mr O K Bwefinora, WCC Ltd managers past and present. I am also grateful to Mr Harry Moss, formerly of Lemco, for kind assistance.

For help in typing an often illegible manuscript I am especially indebted to Karen Johnson and Shirley Fenner. Finally thanks go to my wife Steph and my son Doug for putting up with the times I was away in the bush, for their company on other trips to Hwange and their support with this marathon!

Special thanks to Louise Grantham for giving life to the project and Kate Rogan and the rest of the staff of Southern Books for giving it shape, form and continuity. I am most grateful.

Foreword

The future of Africa's wildlife relies on our understanding of the complexities of nature in all its facets.

Africa has produced many memorable books, but few can have explored the wildlife, ecology and issues of one area in such intimate detail as in *Hwange: Retreat of the Elephants.*

Nick Greaves' painstaking research and fundamental understanding of his subject combine to give us a marvellously complete picture of one of the last great refuges for wildlife left on earth.

Building up layer upon layer, using words and photographs, Hwange and its flora and fauna are revealed in their entire, breathtaking magic. Only a person who has spent years in the field could speak with such authority and passion.

But *Hwange: Retreat of the Elephants* is not only a marvellous tale of nature and natural history. As wildlife and wild places face increasing pressure from human activities around the world, the book clearly stakes Hwange's claim as a site of vital global significance that demands our attention, care and support.

Seen in this light it is all the more disturbing to learn of the problems faced by some of the animals in what should be one of the best protected sanctuaries on earth.

Black rhino, beset on all sides throughout Africa, have not escaped the poacher's murderous attentions in Hwange. The white rhino population has fared little better.

However, it is Hwange's role as a haven and refuge for elephants that forms the core of this fascinating book. Detailed research into elephant biology, their role within the natural habitat, family society and their social structure create a natural history backdrop against which is set the mass slaughter of Africa's elephants that scandalised the 1970s and 1980s.

Nick Greaves untangles the intrigues, power-politics and vested interests that fought to destroy or save the elephant and which led to the CITES International Ivory Trade Ban in 1989.

Now, with the ban in place, the battle lines have been shifted slightly. Some wildlife managers advocate long-term culling of elephants to maintain numbers at predetermined levels — and with the ivory being traded, ostensibly to raise funds for conservation. Others regard such a brutal attempt to control elephant numbers as little more than a 'stalking horse' for the pro-ivory trade lobby.

Hwange: Retreat of the Elephants is compelling, informative, disturbing and delightful. Anyone interested in wildlife, and above all elephants, cannot fail to be persuaded by the important role played by one of Africa's great wildlife sanctuaries — and become convinced that we should do all in our power to protect it and its inhabitants for the future.

William Travers
ELEFRIENDS and
The Born Free Foundation

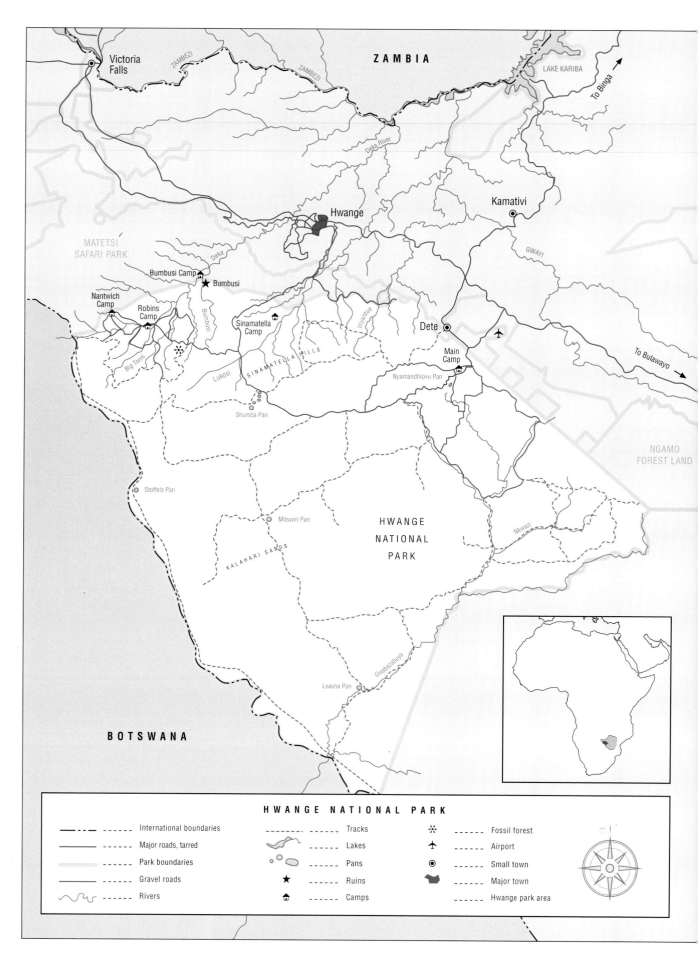

INTRODUCTION

*This we know: the earth does not belong to man, man belongs
to the earth. All things are connected like the blood that unites us all.*

Chief Seattle of the Suquamish: 1854

Situated in the north-western corner of Zimbabwe, abutting the border with Botswana, Hwange National Park is the nation's largest wildlife area and contains the greatest diversity of animal and bird species. Covering 14 540 km² or 1 462 000 hectares, Hwange is roughly the same size as Belgium. Though the park itself is a vast area of wilderness, the peripheral buffer of wildlife utilisation areas, comprising Forestry Commission hunting and photographic areas, National Parks controlled hunting areas, commercial safari hunting concessions, Kazuma Pans National Park and the Zambezi National Park, adds a huge area of more or less continuous land devoted to wildlife. Add to this private commercial farmland being converted back to wildlife and further afield the huge national parks of Chobe, Savuti and Moremi in Botswana,

and Hwange can be considered the nucleus of a vast radiating network dedicated to the various forms of wildlife utilisation.

In fact, the Hwange to Moremi complex could become one of the world's largest, most diverse and most spectacular areas for wildlife, provided the two countries concerned can cooperate to make it so. The infrastructure exists as a sound foundation that could be built on for the benefit of the economies, people and rich wildlife heritage of both countries.

National parks should not be regarded as areas of land wasted by being put aside for the benefit of the wild animals and the rich tourists who come to view, photograph and, on occasion, shoot them. These dry, dusty tracts of lands blighted by low rainfall provide us with a workshop where we can learn more about wildlife and represent a far

Left: *Hwange National Park.* Above: *In the harsh bronze light of an October sunset, a group of
wildebeest plod laboriously from a waterhole on their way to find grazing.*

Left: *A leopard drinks, unperturbed by the presence of a vehicle full of tourists.* Below: *The last light sets clouds aglow at Masuma Dam.*

more productive means of long-term land use than other commercial land-use alternatives. The dry, brittle grasses of Hwange's sandveld contain twice as much crude protein as alternative cultivated fodder crops. This bounty is used by a highly varied biomass of browsing, foraging and grazing creatures, adapted by millions of years of evolution to utilise resources on a sustained-yield basis and at various levels. The same cannot be said of the destructive feeding habits of domestic livestock with far lower diversity and totals of species within the biomass.

Hwange has huge herds of elephant, and is one of the last wilderness areas where they can still be viewed and enjoyed. But Hwange has far, far more. Buffalo, eland, wildebeest, zebra and impala also form large herds and are regularly seen at the many large waterholes. The evocative roar of lions at night adds the thrill of adventure and the sight of a pride on a kill draws thousands of tourists each year; yet Hwange also offers sightings of the endangered African wild dog, the elusive, secretive leopard and the lithe, speedy cheetah. Hwange is famous for its giraffe, and the Main Camp area boasts the highest density of giraffe per square kilometre in Africa. Hwange is also a mecca for birdwatchers with more than 400 species on record — over two-thirds of the total species count for Zimbabwe.

Hwange is well serviced by tourist facilities and roads to many of the major pans. The 480 km of road, of which only 80 km are tarred, are not in the best state of repair at present. However, the Department of National Parks and Wildlife Management will in future be converted into a parastatal body, with an increased level of autonomy and recourse to the huge sums of money it generates each year. This should improve facilities and allow management projects to be reinstated. It has recently been announced that funds will be forthcoming to upgrade roads and facilities in time for the 1997 CITES meeting in Harare. All this will mean a new lease of life for Hwange and all of Zimbabwe's national parks.

A brief history

Hwange was proclaimed a game reserve in 1928, largely because this vast wilderness was regarded as useless for any other purpose. The area's wildlife was virtually hunted out and its only human inhabitants were a few bands of San or Bushmen, hunter-gatherers who had learned to live in harmony with this harsh environment, and commercial poachers who were endangering the last few remaining elephant.

A 22-year-old ranger was installed as first warden of the then Wankie Game Reserve in September 1928. Ted Davidson had the great fortune to nurture and develop Hwange from

Above: *Guvalala Platform is an excellent spot for seeing large gatherings of elephant, mostly bulls, in daylight hours. Here a large bull saunters off after drinking his fill.*

embryo to near-maturity over the next 34 years. During the first two years Davidson and his handful of rangers, armed with antiquated Martini Henry rifles and five rounds of ammunition apiece, covered virtually every square kilometre of the reserve. The lack of game was all too evident — days could be spent on horseback, or foot patrol, with no sight of a single living animal.

The first two decades' work in the park included the back-breaking construction of a road network to allow the first intrepid visitors limited access. Accommodation had to be built for these visitors and rustic huts were erected at Main Camp — the nucleus of the huge complex there today. During these early years, the park was increased in size to its present extent by the addition of several farms, which the Rhodesian government exchanged for new farms elsewhere. The extension of

the reserve into the hills drained by the Deka and Lukosi rivers was a priority to ensure that wildlife could travel safely to the only reliable water sources during the dry season, without running the gauntlet of shooting galleries.

One of the characters associated with Hwange's early days was H G Robins, who took up the farms Big Tom and Little Tom in 1914. (The farms were named after two tributaries of the Deka River.) This diminutive eccentric was undoubtedly a thorn in Ted Davidson's side for although he ranched cattle to start with, subsidising his income by shooting game (a giraffe skin brought the princely sum of five shillings!) he eventually sold off most of his cattle and set up a private game reserve. Visitors to his private domain were faced, on arrival, by a daunting pack of Great Danes, which were locked away for the duration of their visit. One of the old man's pas-

sions was astronomy and he built himself a three-storey tower for an observatory. His strange attire — a large knitted cap and pyjama tops — earned him the nickname 'Gnome'.

As the road system expanded the tracks were extended past Detema and linked up to the Toms Farms, but the old man resented this intrusion into his reserve and had a huge trench dug across the track shortly before his death in 1939. Luckily no one came to any harm in this malicious trap and, as part of the land exchange, the Toms Farms private game sanctuary was incorporated into Hwange. Robins Camp was built and named in remembrance of this crusty old man, one of the early conservationists.

With the first boreholes being sunk in 1939, the water supply programme slowly gained momentum and accordingly the wildlife began to proliferate, slowly building up to the magnificent spectacle we can appreciate today.

Two of the early boreholes were put in at Big Tom and Little Tom on H G Robins' old sanctuary and a small viewing hide was built at each waterhole.

Human presence in the park dates back many thousands of years. The nomadic San left behind some superb engravings on the walls of natural rock shelters in the Bumbusi area as a record of their habitation. Several of these cool shelters have incredibly detailed animal and bird spoors meticulously chipped into the sandstone rockfaces, which have been protected from weathering so that we can still easily identify the individual species. Giraffe, kudu, elephant, lion, wildebeest, warthog and even guineafowl spoor are all that remain of these diminutive hunter-gatherers of the late Stone Age Wilton complex between 20 000 and 10 000 years ago.

The time and effort invested in such intricate decorations indicates that they had great

Above: *Sunset at Imbiza Pan*. Below: *A breed herd moves out of the forest, silhouetted against the dust stirred up by their heavy steps.*

significance in daily ritual, especially those associated with the hunt. Other evidence of San activities was an old well found near the Nehimba Seeps in the Kalahari sands, obviously a vital source of water in these thirsty lands and predictable when all else failed.

Also at Bumbusi and at Mtoa there are rock structure ruins dating from the early 1800s. For a short time Bantu pastoralists set up stone ramparts to build their mud and pole huts on raised platforms. These communities were established in rocky areas which were easy to defend against man and beast alike.

This was the era of the Mfecane, a Nguni word meaning 'to crush', which was set in fearsome motion by the paramountcy of Shaka Zulu, far away on the Natal coast. The war machine of Shaka, his highly disciplined and regimented impis, started a ripple effect that grew to seismic proportions of conquest and annihilation that spread terror across the subcontinent.

The Matabele were a breakaway clan from the yoke of Shaka's oppression led by Mzilikazi, one of his favoured proteges. They arrived in southern Zimbabwe and spread the terror of the Mfecane ever further afield, holding sway over most of Zimbabwe and Botswana for decades.

The early pastoralists deserted the Bumbusi and Mtoa areas soon after, mainly because the land had been over-utilised, but also from fear of Matabele raiding parties. Until the end of the 19th century Hwange was the royal hunting reserve of Mzilikazi and his equally ruthless successor, Lobengula.

It was only after the arrival of the white hunters and the first of the white settlers in the late 1800s that the wildlife was hunted mercilessly, although the Matabele placed heavy pressure on elephants in their areas of control. Ivory was extensively traded with the Arab slavers who used the Zambezi as their highway into the African hinterland. Arabs presented Mzilikazi with 400 old Tower muskets to ensure a constant supply of ivory, and each healthy slave was required to carry an elephant tusk to the coast. The cost of the slave trade in terms of human life cannot even be guessed at; the parallel trade in ivory put pressure on elephant populations in many areas and the large bulls with heavy ivory were the first to go, depleting the breeding pool.

The legendary Frederick Courtney Selous often hunted this area, leaving his oxwagons and horses at a base camp at Linkwasha and travelling on foot to the hilly areas around the Deka to do most of his hunting. The threat of the tsetse fly — now long eradicated from the vicinity — meant that only salted horses, or those immune to the tsetse fly's bite, could enter any fly area. In those days a salted horse was literally worth its weight in gold. Whilst camped on the Dete Vlei near today's Sikumi Tree Lodge, Selous recorded white rhino, but none were left at the time of the Reserve proclamation in 1928. Another famous hunter to operate in this area was Tom Sadler who in 1875 camped between the two small streams which he was to name Big Tom and Little Tom, in the area later owned by H G Robins.

Most of the hunting was carried out in the hills of the Deka/Lukosi drainage system, where game concentrated because of the more reliable year-round water supplies. This depletion was uncontrolled and the area's main breeding pools were seriously threatened by the time the reserve was proclaimed. Poaching continued to be a problem for some time, but regular patrols and permanent ranger posts around the park led to a series of arrests which, in turn, led to fines and convictions. This gradually brought commercial poaching to a halt. Subsistence poaching has always been a problem, particularly along the southern boundary and along the Botswana border. During Zimbabwe's war of liberation, subsistence poaching was encouraged by the local freedom fighters and snaring escalated, in some areas to serious levels. With independence in 1980, hostilities ceased and the new rulers had to re-educate the park's neighbours not to wantonly snare and destroy game. The people were encouraged to see it rather as a vital resource and long-term supplier of much needed hard currency, essential for Zimbabwe's growth and development. The implementation of Operation Campfire nearly a decade later allowed the park's surrounding communities to partake in these financial gains, thus showing the locals the benefits of wildlife to them and their descendants.

In 1949 the National Parks Act upgraded Hwange from a game reserve to the status of a fully sanctioned National Park, secured by law as part of Zimbabwe's natural heritage for ever.

A GEOLOGICAL HISTORY

'What now remains compared with what then
existed is like the skeleton of a sick man, all the fat and
soft earth having been washed away and only the bare
framework of the land being left.'

Plato

Hwange's present structure and landscape is the result of elemental forces set on course countless millions of years ago. The geology and geomorphology of Hwange are the building blocks with which natural forces have moulded what we see now. The Hwange of today is a small moment in time: a frozen frame of an endless motion picture.

Our earliest knowledge of life on earth dates back some 3 000 million years to sim-ple bacteria preserved in flintlike rocks called chert. For many millions of years life was restricted to the warm primeval oceans. Only some 420 million years ago did algae first attempt to colonise the land mass of the single super-continent known as Pangaea. This early colonisation was only possible because of the cooling of the earth's climate, though conditions would have been harsh in the extreme. Invasion of the land only

---

Left: *Countryside typical of the Sinamatella area — black cotton vleis, mopane woodland and flat-topped hills.* Above: *A section of fossilised tree trunk of the species* Dadoxylon, *near Detema, dates back some 200 million years.*

began in earnest some 350 million years ago as fish began to haul themselves out onto dry land, much like the mudskipper of the mangrove swamps.

In these early primeval times, known in geological terms as the Devonian Period, there was less than half as much free atmospheric oxygen as in today's atmosphere. Substantially lower levels of ozone meant higher levels of ultraviolet light which led to rapid genetic mutation, resulting in a proliferation of genetic variation.

Palaeomagnetism shows that the southern African section of Pangaea was over the South Pole at the time and this era of glaciation was far longer and far more severe than the more recent ones in the northern hemisphere.

With the warming of the climate in the Permian Period, which started 280 million years ago, the colonisation of southern Africa by warm-climate life forms started in earnest. During this Permian era the Wankie coal seams were deposited from vast tundra-like cold-climate forests. The gradual warming of the climate led to a massive development of land plants. Fossil trees belonging to the species *Dadoxylon* can be seen in Hwange in the Bumbusi/Detema areas, and are estimated to be 200 million years old. They are evidence of a warmer, arid climate when forests were claimed by advancing sand dunes and silica replacement of the woody structure left behind the internal structure of these ancient tree trunks.

Rocks found in the northern third of Hwange date to this era. They are known as the Karoo System and are primarily sedimentary rocks. Prior to the Karoo System, the

Above: *Open grassland areas surrounded by stands of teak trees typify the Kalahari sands.*

topography left behind by receding glaciers was somewhat similar to today's landscape. The period of glaciation scoured the basement rocks of granite and gneiss and the resultant debris, or tillites, started a long period of sedimentation deposits. The white sandstones around Bumbusi mark the early stages of deposition some 260 million years ago. Cooler conditions and a swampy tundra environment produced the shales and coal deposits in the region and around 200 million years ago the hotter, arid climate produced the desert conditions which preserved the *Dadoxylon* trees. The Karoo Succession drew to an end with weathering reducing the average land elevation to about 800 m above sea level. This period of weathering and prolonged sedimentation was interrupted by the occasional outpouring of basalt, an igneous rock which spewed out from far beneath the earth's surface to cover the sediments.

These basalt extrusions offered a thin protective capping to the more easily eroded sedimentary rocks and gave rise to flat-topped hills bounded by abrupt scarps as seen in the Sinamatella/Hwange area. The final act of the Karoo Succession, about 190 million years ago, was a massive outpouring of basalt, which covered vast areas of southern Africa. The forces responsible for such a cataclysmic rending of the earth's crust to allow huge volumes of molten magma to cover the surface for thousands of square kilometres are beyond the imagination. Over the course of several million years, basalt accumulated to over 9 000 m in depth in places and drastically altered the surface topography. This basalt shield is most spectacularly depicted by the gorges below Victoria Falls where the river has cut down through four major periods of lava flows. The depth of the original deposit is unknown, but it is well over 1 000 m.

The herculean forces which unleashed these massive deposits signalled the breakup of ancient Pangaea. The landmass started to separate into two distinct supercontinents, Laurasia (which consisted of North America, Europe and northern Asia) and Gondwanaland (South America, Africa, southern Asia, Antarctica and Australia). The continents were akin to a series of buoyant mats floating on a seething mass of molten magma.

With the separation of major sections of the continental crust, drastic changes in the planet's weather patterns were set in motion. A period of favourable conditions allowed the development of many new plant species to add to the growing variation and richness of life. This was the Jurassic Period, the golden age of the dinosaur and the first stage of the development of the earliest mammals. As time progressed, subterranean forces caused further breakup of the continental crusts about 110 million years ago, and gradually the outlines of today's continents became discernible, though they only obtained their current forms some 10 million years ago.

The African section of Gondwanaland has been the most stable of all the crustal components and has changed the least in terms of latitude in the past 150 million years. All of today's ancestors of the African bush, plant and animal, have developed in relative isolation and in favourable conditions.

The Kalahari sands

The southern two-thirds of the park are covered in an ancient detritus, a blanket of sand and gravel comparatively young in age, but whose genesis is far more ancient. The Kalahari sands, which form the world's largest continuous sand body, extend over some 2 million km². The age of the Kalahari is difficult to ascertain, but it is believed to be about 65 million years old, dating from the early Tertiary Period. Certain areas within the Kalahari have isolated pockets of newer deposits, some as recent as 2 million years old. The evolution of the Kalahari coincided with the sudden worldwide die-off of the dinosaurs.

It is not known precisely where all the sand required to cover an area of over 2 million km² to a depth of between 20 m and 300 m came from. The Kalahari sands are basically aeolian deposits, i.e. an accumulation of windblown sand and dust. In Hwange the Kalahari sands cover the same Karoo bedrocks that are exposed in the northern third of the park.

In the 120 million years following its extrusion, the massive basalt shield was constantly under attack in a process known as pediplanation — the remorseless action of wind, rain, heat and cold gradually wore away a surface rock kilometres thick in places, leaving behind isolated patches of remnant basalt shield.

Above left: *A bull elephant coated in Kalahari sand from a post-bathe dusting down*. Above right: *Before the rains the Kalahari sands form miniature dunes, seemingly barren and devoid of life*. Right: *A female kudu pauses while licking essential minerals from the calcrete rock deposits around Guvalala Pan*.

Robins Camp is situated on the edge of the Matetsi Shield, which spreads beyond Victoria Falls and into Zambia. Put in simplistic model form, the southern African subcontinent is similar to a shallow dish raised around the edges with a huge shallow depression in the interior. Millions of cubic metres of rock were worn down to sand grains. With insufficient runoff owing to the lower rainfall, the sands and gravels were not washed away into the oceans. Rivers and lakes clogged and silted and the remaining deposits were blown around by the prevailing winds.

This blanket of Kalahari sands has been reshaped since its original deposition by a succession of wet and dry eras. One example is best seen from the air, as only from this elevation do the remains of 'fossil' sand dunes become evident. During long, arid spells the wind blew the sand into a series of parallel sand dunes aligned east–west and now seldom more than 20 m in height with crests about 1,5 km apart. These fossil dunes are now anchored by vegetation, primarily teak forest, and are in places bisected by dry river courses which cut through the dunes in wetter pluvial periods in more recent times. The fossil riverbeds attest to cooler, wetter periods as recent as 1 500 years ago, draining the Kalahari sands out to the former inland sea of Lake Makgadikgadi, which is now a dry, lifeless, salt-flat depression. Certainly wetter conditions have been a feature of the last 10 million years, again due to continental drift pushing the Antarctic to its present polar position, allowing circumpolar air movements to the benefit of southern Africa.

The only recent geological feature found in the Kalahari sands of Hwange is a rock deposit called calcrete. Calcrete consists mainly of lime precipitated from soil water. Rainwater becomes saturated in carbonates produced by chemical weathering. As it percolates through the sands some is deposited below the surface and, in effect, cements the soil together. In areas where calcrete lies close to the surface, the wildlife will dig or scrape to these layers and use the calcrete as a salt lick to obtain essential minerals.

CHAPTER 3

VEGETATION

*'Among the scenes which are deeply impressed
on my mind, none exceed in sublimity the primal forests
undefaced by the hand of man ... no-one can stand in these
solitudes unmoved, and not feel there is more in man
than the mere breath of his body.'*

Charles Darwin

Hwange is classified as an area of mixed woodlands and open savanna — a cartographer's classification that does no justice to the diversity and variety of the area. Hwange's vegetation, so important for sustaining the basic cycle of life within the animal, bird, reptile and insect communities, is highly varied, with 1 070 plant species identified to date. Of this total, 255 species of trees and shrubs dominate large tracts of land in the park, but the 202 species of grasses form the most easily accessible food for most of the herbivores.

The distribution of the main vegetation groups in Hwange is controlled by soil type rather than by any other factor. Again the park can be divided into two zones — one to the south of the watershed on the Kalahari sands, which at all times seem hard to classify as 'soils', and the other to the north of the watershed on the more variable clayey and mixed soils.

Left: *The famous upside-down trees of Africa, the baobabs, grow to gigantic proportions.*
Above: *Flowers of the shaving-brush combretum.*

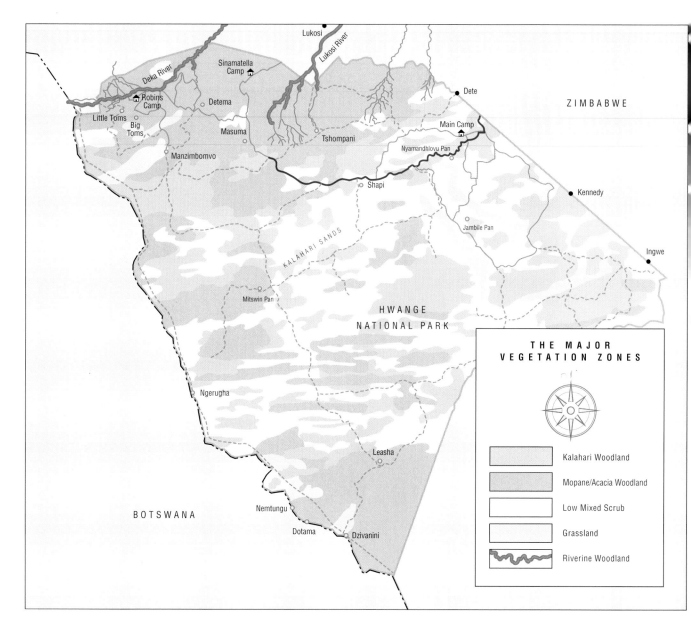

THE MAJOR VEGETATION ZONES

Kalahari Woodland

Mopane/Acacia Woodland

Low Mixed Scrub

Grassland

Riverine Woodland

Kalahari woodland

The large area of Kalahari sands, which covers two-thirds of the park, usually has deep soils, so the dominant tree species can grow deep, extensive root systems. The dominant species are Zambezi teak (*Baikiaea plurijuga*), mukwa (*Pterocarpus angolensis*), and umtshibi (*Guibortia coleosperma*), which form large stands of woodland and open woodland. The understorey in these woodlands consists largely of flowering shrubs and legumes such as *Baphia*, *Croton*, *Grewia* and *Combretum*. The lower level of vegetation is dominated by grasses with a large variety of species ranging from unpalatable three-awn grass (*Aristida stipitata*) to highly productive forage such as Guinea grass (*Panicum maximum*).

The lowest productive level is subterranean and the Kalahari sands harbour a large number of species of bulbous and succulent flowering plants. The roots and stems of these plants are capable of storing large quantities of water, essential in order to survive the long harsh dry season. Families such as *Euphorbiaceae*, *Liliaceae*, *Iridaceae*, *Amaryllidaceae* and *Asclepiadaceae* sometimes store water over a metre below the surface, a fact that enabled the San to survive in this area long after the rains had finished. A great number of animals, especially rodents such as porcupine and springhare, dig up the bulbs to get at their moisture in the dry season.

The teak is the dominant or climax vegetation in these woodlands. These medium to large hardwood trees, 8 to 16 m in height, are characterised by large spreading crowns and, although they are deciduous, the foliage is retained for a good proportion of the year and turns a golden yellow before dropping. The leaves are not very nutritious; only elephant and giraffe seem to utilise them and then in no particular preference to other plants. The large mauve flowers sprout in the latter part of the rainy season and giraffe, baboon and many species of birds seem to enjoy them. The flattened, woody pods are covered in brown, velvety hair and are fed upon by a large number of animals, including elephant, eland, duiker, vervet monkey, baboon and many rodents. A characteristic sound of these teak forests in August and September is the explosive splitting of the seed pods — nature ensuring the seeds are well dispersed by being flung some distance from the parent tree.

The umtshibi or large-leaved false mopane is a medium to large tree with a fine rounded crown, but with a smoother, creamy bark which is much favoured by elephant and distinguishes it from the teak. The flowers are small and creamy white and the pods, with a single large seed, are much sought after by many animals and birds, particularly the various hornbills. The seeds were an important staple food for the nomadic San people who used to roam Hwange's sandveld. The seeds were roasted under the coals of their campfires and then pounded and cooked to be eaten as meal.

The mukwa is also a large tree with a flat canopy, but unlike the teak and umtshibi it does not retain its foliage for up to nine months of the year. The flat, circular pods are

Above left: *The brilliant blooms of the Zambezi gold appear when the rains arrive, transforming an otherwise small, nondescript shrub.*
Above: *The delicate flower of the white bauhinia adds a splash of colour to this untidy, rangy bush.*
Left: *The porcupine, Africa's largest rodent, lives off the bulbs and roots found in the soil in the dry season.*

Above: *A lone camel-thorn at sunset.*

highly distinctive as the centre is covered in harsh bristles and surrounded by a wavy, membranous wing. The mukwa or kiaat is one of the best known and most used trees in southern Africa and the hard termite and borer resistant wood is made into dishes, mortars, drums, dugout canoes, game and fish spears and canoe paddles. Decoctions of bark and root make the mukwa a regular bush dispensary as they are used in cures for ailments ranging from corneal ulcers to ringworm, malaria and gonorrhoea.

Some parts of the Kalahari are covered in a more mixed open woodland with a greater variation of species, including *Terminalia, Combretum, Ochna* and *Bauhinia*. The Kalahari Christmas tree (*Dichrostachys cinerea*) can often form thick impenetrable stands which research has shown to be self-sustaining.

Vegetation is not inanimate, but is involved in a constant struggle for supremacy against competitors. The *Dichrostachys* keeps one step ahead of the pack by releasing toxins from its root system which inhibit germination in competitors.

The red syringa (*Burkea africana*) is a medium-sized tree growing up to 10 m in height and common in places. The syringa is distinctive as clusters of seed pods remain on the treetops long after the leaves have fallen.

The loamy soils found on the Kalahari sands can form large, open grasslands and vleis and are usually associated with subterranean calcrete deposits. The diversity of grass species ensures good grazing conditions for large numbers of herbivores. These grassy areas can have patches of *Combretum* and *Terminalia* scrub and, in the main depression areas such as

Above: *A lone camel-thorn at sunset.*

in Hwange. These large, flat-topped trees are invaluable as a source of shade, and their seed pods are excellent fodder that are keenly sought after by elephants, which eat large quantities of pods and widely disperse vast numbers of ready-to-germinate seeds in their dung. Many other animals and birds seek out the seeds from such dung piles as they are far easier to obtain in this manner than to extract them from the hard pods.

Recent research has shown that many acacia species have a self-defence mechanism to protect them from over-utilisation by browsing species. The tree is able to produce extra tannins when it senses it is being damaged by too much browsing. These tannins are concentrated in the branches being browsed and make the foliage less palatable and harder to digest. This chemical defence is not only deployed by individual trees under threat; other trees in the vicinity can respond to one tree's increase in tannin production by stepping up their levels as well. This remarkable defence mechanism ensures that browsers do not place too much strain on the plant's life support system and forces them to move off to other areas and food types.

Mopane woodland

The northern third of the park has its own regime of tree species. The varying geology of basalts, shales, sandstones and granite-gneiss complex gives a greater variety of shallow soil types, but true mopane (*Colophospermum mopane*) dominates the region. Depending on the soil depth the mopane varies from stunted scrub 4 m in height to large 18 m trees. The mopane's tolerance of alkaline and poorly drained soils ensures a wide distribution throughout south tropical Africa. The butterfly-shaped leaves droop or close during the heat of the day to cut down on transpiration and preserve moisture. These leaves are important fodder for the wildlife as they are very high in protein, whether fresh on the twig or dry and windblown. The large vivid caterpillar of the mopane moth (*Gonimbrasia belina*) swarms in countless thousands during good rainy seasons. Despite the garish and alarming appearance of these caterpillars, they are packed with fats and protein and are eagerly sought after as food by many animals,

Ngamo, Makololo and Mbiza, the northern ilala palm (*Hyphaene benguellensis*) with its much sought after vegetable ivory fruits, is common. An important shrub species is the wild gardenia (*Gardenia spatulifolia*) with its beautifully scented flowers. It is heavily browsed on by many species, especially giraffe.

Acacia woodlands often border the vlei and grassland areas and form large, shady stands. Acacia species include *Acacia tortilis*, the characteristic umbrella thorn, *A. fleckii* or bladethorn which, as its name suggests, is evilly armed and can form such impenetrable thickets that even elephants cannot push through, and *A. luederitzii*, the Kalahari sand acacia, with its swollen mature spines, which also forms thickets. *Acacia erioloba* or camelthorn (a mistranslation from the Afrikaans for 'giraffe thorn') is probably the best-known thorn tree especially birds. In poor rural areas, these caterpillars are an important source of food for humans and are eaten fresh or sun dried for storage.

One of Africa's most distinctive trees, the baobab (*Adansonia digitata*), is found in the northern part of Hwange. The smooth, grey bark, squat, large trunk and stubby splayed branches gave rise to the myth that the trees are actually upside down. One of Africa's most utilised trees, the baobab is steeped in legend and superstition. An infusion of bark, when consumed, is supposed to act as protection from crocodile attack, whilst anyone foolhardy enough to pluck a baobab flower – believed by many tribes to be inhabited by spirits — will be devoured by a lion! Large baobab specimens are believed to be over 3 000 years old. Elephants often gouge chunks out of the trunk as it is soft, pulpy and full of moisture and at certain times of the year is a vital source of trace elements. The baobab is unique in the tree world as it is the only species capable of withstanding ring-barking, which is often the result of extensive feeding pressure by elephant. The large white, waxy flowers open mostly at night and are pollinated by fruit bats. The pods are packed with seeds and a white, powdery pulp which is full of tartaric acid and potassium bitartrate, refreshing to both man and beast.

Grassland

Expanses of black cotton soil support other extensive areas of grassland in the northern area of the park with a large variety of grass species. Of particular note are the thatching grasses (*Hyparrhenia*), which can grow to more than 2 m in height and are very poor in nutritional value, but very good at reducing visibility to virtually nil! These black cotton soils form sticky expanses which bog down even the sturdiest four-wheel-drive vehicle during the rains and these areas — particularly in the Robins Camp vicinity — are closed to the public during the rains. Leadwood (*Combretum imberbe*) commonly fringes such grassy areas.

Riverine woodland

Another vegetation type found in the northern part of the park is riverine woodland. Here the only large rivers are to be found, the Lukosi and Deka, which comprise the main drainage systems. The rich alluvial soils that line the rivers support dense vegetation and large trees such as the monkeythorn (*Acacia galpinii*), the aptly named splendid acacia (*Acacia robusta*) and the well-armed knobthorn (*Acacia nigrescens*). Other large trees include the sausage tree (*Kigelia africana*), whose large polony-shaped fruit can weigh up to 10 kg.

Left: *A kudu bull, the grey ghost of Africa, stands motionless in a barren stand of mopane near Sinamatella.*
Above: *Elephant wander through a magnificent stand of* Acacia erioloba *in search of the delicious seed pods that fall from these trees.*

Campers are advised not to set up tent beneath these appealing shady trees for obvious reasons! The large purple flowers of the *Kigelia* are rich in nectar and, like the baobab, are often pollinated by bats.

The African ebony (*Diospyros mespiliformis*) is another large shady tree and is far more suitable for camping underneath. The small fleshy fruit is eagerly sought after by animals and birds and the tree parts are widely used in many traditional cures.

The broken hilly area of granite-gneiss koppies is not visited much owing to lack of usable tourist roads. The shallow sandy soils support a mixed woodland predominantly of mopane and mfuti or Prince of Wales feathers (*Brachystegia boehmii*), another valuable shade tree, noted for its durable bark rope. Another feature of the vegetation in this area, apart from baobabs, is the very pale-barked tick tree or African star chestnut (*Sterculia africana*). The fruit pods are inedible and fringed with fine bristles, reminiscent of ticks, and the tree produces an excruciatingly itchy powder.

The many types of vegetation and myriad different species of trees, shrubs and grasses all contribute to the uniqueness of Hwange. Add to this the profusion of colourful flowers during the rainy season and the variation between areas and seasons becomes even greater. This contrast is quickly evident to even the most casual observer as in places a few kilometres of travel can take one from mature woodlands of ancient teak, through open grasslands and on into mopane and *Terminalia* scrub. This wide range of plant life allows the development of many diverse niches and ecosystems, making Hwange home to creatures ranging from the most primitive lichens on rock faces, to complex and sophisticated parasitic orchids.

CLIMATE

*'Nature gives to every time and season some beauties
of its own: and from morning to night, as from the cradle
to the grave, is but a succession of changes so gentle and
easy that we can scarcely mark the progress.'*

Charles Dickens

The marked contrast in the climate between Hwange's various seasons brings many variations to its character. Summer and winter do not fall neatly in line with the wet and dry seasons. Furthermore, visitors from outside the region must remember that the seasons are opposite to those in the northern hemisphere — a significant factor when considering what to pack!

The dry season

During the winter anti-cyclonic conditions establish themselves over the subcontinent and Hwange's days are characterised by fine sunny weather, clear, rainless skies and light south-easterly winds. During the winter months of May to August, when ambient temperatures are mainly regulated by an average altitude of 1 000 m above sea level, dry cloudless skies can lead to dramatic temperature variations created by the rapid loss of heat through thermal radiation.

Though daytime temperatures regularly sit around the 25-28 °C mark and at times even exceed 30 °C, night-time temperatures soon plummet and ground frosts are not uncommon. The lowest recorded minimum ground temperature was a chilling -14,4 °C in August 1972 during a severe black frost.

Left: *Storm clouds start to gather, forming spectacular cloudscapes.* Above: *Pans begin to dry up as the long, hot dry season takes its toll.*

Though this is an extreme example, the temperature regularly falls to freezing point in places, especially along vleis. Visitors to Hwange in the winter months should be equipped with warm clothing for the evenings, especially if going on night or early morning game drives.

Black frosts occur about once every four years and the effect on vegetation can be dramatic. A harsh black frost can severely damage or even kill woody shrubs and young trees and much of the park's vegetation shows the ravages of such frosts in past years. Tree species such as mukwa (*Pterocarpus angolensis*), teak (*Baikiaea plurijuga*) and various *Combretums* are particularly susceptible to black frosts.

At times high-pressure systems off the KwaZulu-Natal coast can cause an influx of drab, unpleasant cloud and strong south-easterly winds, but average sunshine is nine hours a day in winter — a pleasant feature to visitors from Europe, in particular.

The rainy season

The hot, dry months of September and October also have marked variations in temperature, but the extremes move to higher levels. The winds shift to a north-easterly direction, owing to the southward shift of the equatorial low-pressure belt and the subsequent subtropical anti-cyclones developing over the southern Indian Ocean. This causes cloud cover to increase and evening temperatures rise well above freezing point. Lack of substantial cloud cover during the day causes ground temperatures to soar into the upper 30s, even topping 40 °C at times.

The rainy season usually commences in November as the subcontinent experiences the effect of monsoonal evaporation from the southern Indian Ocean. In Hwange, as with most of Zimbabwe, the early rains usually come in the form of local thunderstorms, sometimes of frightening intensity, created by the convectional instability typical of large land masses. Tropical cyclones spread monsoonal inflow to the region from December to March and the Inter-Tropical Convergence Zone creates most of the season's rains.

Hwange's rainfall is unreliable, as is the case with most of the subcontinent's interior. Average rainfall is about 640 mm per annum, though the variation can be huge, with a minimum recorded in 1923/24 of 361,8 mm and a maximum in 1973/74 of 1 159,8 mm. The mean average of rainy days per annum is 74 days, but such statistics do not give an indication of the variability of rain in different areas of the park.

The spectre of drought constantly haunts southern Africa and Hwange shows a statistical average of drought one year in five. The distribution of rain and its subsequent runoff

Far left: *A lack of funds to repair faulty, ageing borehole pumps has left Amadundumela Pan dry and barren.* Left: *A newly emerged cicada. These insects come out when it rains, having spent up to seven years in their subterranean larval stage.* Above: *Masuma Pan in the dry season. This is one of the pans affected by lack of funds for borehole maintenance.* Right: *A rare occurrence in drought-plagued Hwange — exceptionally heavy rains flood the roads, causing extensive damage.*

to the pans and the more limited river drainage areas in the north-west of the park, can have a very marked effect on the distribution of large herbivores throughout Hwange.

With the start of the rains and the greater degree of cloud cover, daytime temperatures drop to more comfortable levels from the searing heat of October. Temperatures during the rainy season are normally between 30 and 34 °C. As the rains peter out in March and April, daytime and night-time temperatures drop gradually.

Climate can be a factor affecting the enjoyment of a trip to Hwange, especially for visitors from overseas who are unfamiliar with the weather in the region. But it is the harshness of Hwange's climate, the extremes of heat and cold, wet and dry, that help create the park's unmistakable flavour of unspoilt African wilderness.

CHAPTER 5

RETREAT OF THE ELEPHANTS

'About an hour later we came up with them standing some fifty yards away on our right under a clump of camelthorn trees and in a rather open place, compared with the general density of the surrounding jungle. Besides the small troop of bulls we had followed, there was a very large herd of cows, and as we had not crossed their spoor, they had probably drunk at Sikumi.'

Frederick Courtney Selous

Hwange is most famous for its elephants and while they certainly dominate, the park also boasts 107 species of mammals and 410 species of birds (either residents or seasonal migrants). The diversity of species is enhanced by the diversity of the vegetation zones within the park, but these do not, as a rule, demarcate distribution.

The provision of artificial water points has undoubtedly aided wildlife by making sure that life-giving water is available all year round. The bonanza of reliable drinking water has had numerous effects on the animals and their habitat. The seasonal migrations between the park and more reliable sources of water, mainly in the drainage areas to the north and east, are now a thing of the past.

This factor, plus the control of unregulated hunting prior to the establishment of the

---

Left: *A calf reaches out to his mother for comfort at the waterhole.* Above: *Part of the presidential herd feeding peacefully in the teak forest in the fading light of afternoon.*

Left: *A breed herd on its way to a pan makes a formidable road block. Motorists have to be extremely careful when breed herds are around.* Below: *A solitary bull pauses in a grassy glade in the rainy season. During the rains grass forms a staple in the elephants' diet.*

park in 1928, has resulted in a spectacular increase in the population figures of most species. The increase in the elephant population is probably the most remarkable and definitely the most contentious in conservation circles.

The original population of less than 1 000 timid and harassed elephants has grown to a computer-projected population of more than 30 000 animals. Although they have the longest gestation period of any mammal — 22 months — elephants have a very efficient breeding biology and can, if given the chance, reproduce and grow in numbers at a remarkable rate. The numbers were also increased by the introduction of other displaced populations seeking refuge from man's seemingly insatiable demand for land.

Breeding

The breeding biology of the elephant is extremely complex and has taken decades of painstaking research and careful observation to unravel. Because of the long gestation period (the longest of any mammal) the elephant's breeding biology and demographics in the wild are very hard to study accurately and have only recently been detailed at length by researchers such as Dr Iain Douglas-Hamilton in Manyara National Park in Tanzania and Dr Cynthia Moss in Amboseli National Park in Kenya. These studies involved lengthy docu-

mentation and close association with well-defined family units in the relatively confined space of a small national park. Most details of breeding biology have been obtained from the post mortem of cull victims, such as the extensive research carried out by Professor John Hanks in the Luangwa Valley National Park in Zambia.

More than 80 per cent of females come into season and ovulate during the rainy season. It would appear that the change in diet from dry-season browse and dry grass with a low crude protein content, to a more wholesome rainy-season diet of fresh green grass with higher protein levels stimulates ovulation and promotes successful mating. The relationship between conception and rainfall seems to be more pronounced as one moves away from the equator and the rainy season becomes more distinct. The timing of ovulation and conception, and the length of the gestation period, mean that the young are born 22 months later coinciding with the onset of another rainy season.

An animal with the bulk of an elephant conceals pregnancy very well, though the foetus shows all the major elephantine features after only three months of development. The most rapid growth of the foetus occurs in the latter half of the pregnancy and at birth the youngster weighs in at around 120 kg. Usually the first outward sign that a female is pregnant

Below: A rare occurrence — twins born to one of the cows of the presidential herd.

is the swelling of the mammary glands at about 16 months.

An important factor in the elephant's breeding biology and the species' population dynamics is the age at which females start breeding and how often they breed. This crucial fact was learnt from post mortem studies of culled animals and the study of thousands of uteri. The removal of the placenta at birth results in the loss of a considerable amount of maternal tissue, leaving a well-defined scar. Post mortem examination of the scar tissue indicates how many calves the female has borne in her reproductive lifespan, and the calving period of the population is worked out by gauging the females' ages. The occurrence of twins is rare (less than 1% of all births) and does not have a significant effect on calving statistics.

Using these parameters an interesting pat-

tern becomes evident, especially when one correlates the results of different elephant populations around Africa. During the mid-1960s, surveys of two different elephant populations in different areas of Uganda showed that elephants in one area with a density of 0,85 elephant per km^2 were increasing in number at the rate of 8,5 per cent a year. The second study area had a higher density of 1,74 elephant per km^2 and the increment had fallen to less than 6 per cent a year. Again, post mortem results show us that in areas where elephant densities are low, either because of natural stress such as drought, or man-made stress from over-hunting, poaching or culling, elephants start to breed earlier — as young as 12 years of age — and have infants by the age of 14. In areas where elephants live in higher densities, either secure and free from persecution or compressed into restricted areas by loss of range to human competition, females may only ovulate for the first time at 18 or even 20 years of age. Thus environmental or human pressures stimulate a breeding response and not only do they start breeding earlier, but the

frequency of breeding is stepped up. Calving periods can be as short as three years between young, whilst in high-density areas calving periods can extend to six years between young. When transferred to graphs, this variation in rates of reproductivity clearly shows how the elephants can drastically alter their rates of replacement.

At birth there is little or no difference in the size of infant males and females and their growth rates are remarkably similar in their first ten years of life. The smallest infant on record was the hapless victim of a cull, being only a couple of days old and too young to hand-rear successfully. This diminutive but outwardly healthy male weighed just 68 kg.

Only in early adolescence does the difference in sexes start to become evident. Both males and females continue to grow in size and bulk during their lives, though this growth is faster and to a greater extent in the males. Females grow to a shoulder height of about 3 m and weigh up to 4 tons, whilst males grow to a shoulder height of 4 m and weigh up to 6 tons.

Above: *A bull braces the base of his trunk against a camelthorn* (Acacia erioloba)*, using all his weight and strength to set the tree swaying crazily to loosen the seed pods, a favourite food item.*

Feeling

Elephants certainly are spectacular feeders, with an average daily intake of up to 300 kg of food for a large bull. During the course of the year this diet varies considerably. In the wet season grass predominates, whilst leaves, roots, seeds and bark increase in volume as the dry season progresses.

With its considerable height and reach advantage, an elephant may simply push over a whole tree or tear down a large area of its canopy to obtain a mouthful of leaves left behind by browsers of other species. Indigenous trees have adapted to this wasteful habit and species such as the mopane very quickly coppice or re-grow, forming lower, stunted forests. This activity of the elephants brings valuable food resources, previously inaccessible to most other browsers, to a height where many can now utilise them.

Below: During the dry season the elephants' diet consists mainly of rough, protein-poor twigs, sticks and bark. Bottom: Mineral salts are an essential additive in the elephants' diet. They dig up mineral-rich soil with their tusks and throw it to the back of their throats to swallow, as if they knew that chewing such a gritty mixture would increase tooth wear and reduce their lifespan.

Fallen branches and fruits also afford protection to perennial grasses, again providing food and shelter to many animals, birds and reptiles. A tall, cathedral-like grove of mature trees is undoubtedly a beautiful sight, but the biomass it can support is far less than a stand that elephants have utilised, making it available to many other species.

Though elephants are very efficient at obtaining their bulky diet, they are very inefficient in digesting it. Such a high-bulk diet has to pass quickly through the digestive tract and a surprisingly high percentage of the protein and minerals is not recovered, but passed out in the animals' dung. This nutrition may be overlooked by the elephant, but many others are quick to take advantage. Small mammals such as mongooses and many rodents, as well as birds such as hornbills and francolins, quickly home in on fresh elephant dung and glean the abundant pickings, especially undigested seeds.

The main utilisers of elephant dung are undoubtedly insects and it is remarkable to see how quickly dung beetles — members of the scarab family — will locate and congregate at a fresh pile of dung. The dung beetles, which include over 780 species in southern Africa alone, are prodigious utilisers of elephant dung. Their life cycle has evolved to ensure that they can make use of the parts not used by the elephant or any other scavenger. In this process they return nutrients back to the soil and thereby to the cycle of life of the veld.

A single pile of elephant dung can yield thousands of dung beetles ranging in size from 2 mm to 60 mm. The benefit of their actions is legendary. Some species roll nuptial and larval dung balls, many times their size and weight, far away from the original dung pile. The result is that 90 per cent of faecal nitrogen is returned to the soil. In an area the size of Hwange more than 1 400 kg of dung may be buried daily during the dung beetles' active period in the rainy season.

Termites also make a considerable contribution to the recycling process as they alone in the entire animal kingdom are capable of consuming cellulose and lignin. These are the basic building blocks of wood and contain valuable protein and nitrogen, but termites cannot digest these elements by themselves. This amazing feat is done with the help of a

Far left: *A lone bull slakes his thirst at Makololo Pan after a long, hot day feeding in the woodlands.*
Left: *A legion of common dung beetles swarms over fresh elephant dung, performing a vital function in the nutrient cycle.*
Below: *A young cow dexterously uses her trunk to pluck leaves off a knobthorn (Acacia nigrescens).*

fungus called *Termitomyces* and a complex symbiotic relationship whereby the fungus is found only in termite mounds. The termite mounds or nest structures are one of the distinctive features of the African bush, but the spectacular peaks and spires above ground conceal a complex structure designed to regulate temperature and humidity for the fungus gardens deep underground. The fungus is present in the gut of the termite which allows a limited amount of direct digestion, but the faecal remains are nurtured and maintained by special workers to form fungus gardens. It is in these gardens that the breakdown of cellulose is completed and this unique food resource is made available to the colony, often numbering millions of termites.

The massive population of termites cleans up the elephant-damaged tree trunks and branches, as well as their droppings. Termites also utilise trees and vegetation without the help of elephants and their foraging can destroy up to 25 per cent of the veld's annual production of woody structure and foliage — a far higher proportion of utilisation than the elephants of Hwange.

The termites' prodigious success comes full circle as they are a vital and basic element in the food chain and are preyed upon by a multitude of creatures, great and small. One of the annual features of the changing seasons is the nuptial flight of countless millions of winged males and females triggered by the first falls of rain. These sexually active members of the colony, called alates, have the gift of flight for a few short hours to enable them to fly far from the parent colony and pair off to start a new colony of their own. After the first rains the air fills with astonishing numbers of termites. Such a bonanza triggers off a feeding frenzy where it seems that every creature in the bush depends on this meal for its very existence. The short flight ends for a few when they land, shed their two pairs of wings, frantically find a mate and quickly dig what may, with luck, become one of nature's most spectacular communities.

Drinking

Elephants not only consume vast quantities of vegetation, but their digestive processes require large volumes of water. An adult will drink up to 100 litres of water at one sitting. This they are able to do using their master-piece of evolutionary design — their trunk. This remarkably dexterous appendage, which is actually a fusion of their nose and upper lip, is controlled by thousands of muscles and is capable of performing a vast range of tasks including picking up individual seeds, gathering food, pulling down trees and branches, relieving itches, gesturing and communicating, vocalising, and siphoning four to eight litres of water at one go.

Water is not only a basic commodity essential to life, but an obvious joy and source of playful release to an elephant. All elephants revel in water and the stately demeanour of even aged bulls and dowager matriarchs dissolves at the waterhole. Elephants bathe extensively, especially in the heat of the dry season prior to the rains, and here their trunks take on another aspect — that of a snorkel — allowing total submersion. After this joyful dip the elephant uses its trunk to apply a mud pack and 'talc' itself down with dust and sand.

Keeping cool

The elephant's huge bulk creates a problem with thermoregulation and a cooling bath obviously helps the animal shed excess heat. The rough skin of an elephant is deeply pitted and finely channelled, with a surface area over ten times that of an equivalent smooth surface. When the elephant bathes in the pan and then dusts down afterwards, the skin's structure ensures that the drying mud pack traps water, keeping the body cool for longer. The elephant's skin is not equipped with pores and it cannot thermoregulate by sweating as this would result in far too much water loss.

Elephants carry out another vital function in their ablutions and one that is crucial to the existence of places such as Hwange. Their bathing activities are essential for the creation and formation of the very waterholes they depend on for life. Any small depression created by the erosive power of the wind can collect rainwater to form a puddle during a heavy storm. A herd of elephants can stop at this puddle and drink and daub themselves with mud. The weight of the animals compresses the substrata, creating an impermeable seal which enhances water retention and inhibits the perennial grass roots from breaking the seal. Each elephant can carry off several kilograms of mud after a good wallow and mud bath. Given enough time a small pan can become established and the more reliable it becomes as a source of water, the more elephants and other animals visit, creating distinct game trails which radiate outwards. This mosaic of trails help funnel more runoff water into the pan, helping it to become better established.

The elephant's massive ears, which make up nearly one-third of the body's surface area, are heavily laced with blood vessels, especially in the more shaded rear. The languorous flapping of ears in the heat of the day is not a sign of boredom, but another means of thermoregulation. The huge ears act as massive radiators, shedding unwanted body heat into the atmosphere.

Communication

Research conducted by Katherine Payne and Joyce Poole in Amboseli, Kenya, shows how elephants converse with each other over a distance of several kilometres by emitting low-frequency calls, inaudible to the human ear. This infrasound method of communication is similar to that of the other endangered leviathan, the whale. Scientists have yet to discover to what extent elephants communicate, not only with their family group, but with other elephants further afield.

It has been known for some

Below: *A young bull scents the air for signs of possible danger.*

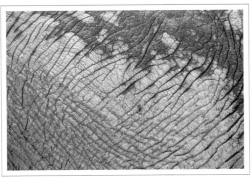

time that elephants can communicate over distances, but the mechanism was not understood. During culling operations, entire family units were killed to reduce the impact of the trauma to those herds that were spared. It seems, however, that this method was ineffective. Infrasound communication means that the anguish and death pangs of a herd being eliminated — no matter how speedily and

Top: *A female and her calf scent the breeze for information from others in the herd, as well as signs of any possible danger.* Above left: *The wrinkled texture of an elephant's hide retains water and assists with thermoregulation.* Above: *A masterpiece of evolution, the elephant's trunk allows the necessary dexterity their massive bodies lack. Here an elephant sucks up water direct from a borehole outlet.*

efficiently — spreads panic from one group to another.

The distress within the population is all too evident during culling, and the normal prolonged social interaction and hedonistic pursuit of pleasure at the waterhole collapses. Frightened animals hang back from waterholes in thick cover, only to steal a quick drink and depart hastily under the safe blanket of darkness. The effect of culling can trigger large-scale migrations away from the cull to the safety of areas across the border in Botswana, or to the sanctuary of the Hwange Safari Lodge estate where culling does not take place. The unease felt by the elephants permeates even to the estate's presidential herd, normally quite at ease in the presence of human beings. Although no elephants have been culled in Hwange for several years, the cull has left its mark on the psyche of the elephant population. A herd of elephant can be milling and cavorting at a waterhole when, in unison, they freeze. A few seconds later the herd will again act as one and flee in silent panic for the treeline and the safety of cover. Several minutes later the dull drone of a light aircraft or helicopter on a rhino population survey will become audible to the human ear. The light aircraft has become the harbinger of death in the elephants' collective memory, a memory that can be passed down intact for generations.

Above: *A couple of bulls greet each other with touches of their trunks.*
Right: *The area around Big Toms Pan is open, cleared of mopane scrub by the elephants — some consider this a devastation while others see it as beneficial to other species.*

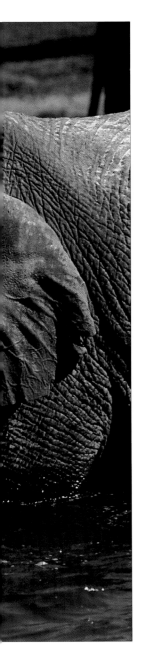

The supreme architects

As we gain more knowledge about all aspects of the ecology of the bush, it becomes apparent that elephants are, or were, the supreme architects of Africa. Over the last 700 years human pressure and the ivory trade gradually depleted elephant populations across the continent. During this period of exploitation the vegetation was spared the normal pressure of elephant feeding, and with our narrow baseline of expertise we tend to regard elephant-free woodlands as the desired 'natural' state of affairs. In reality, elephants have shaped the vegetation of Africa for millions of years with cycles of tree growth, utilisation, depletion and final regeneration corresponding to fluctuations in elephant densities and distributions.

Africa has developed to the extent where its wilderness areas have become isolated oases where biological diversity fights a losing battle against time. Genetic diversity in these increasingly isolated areas of wilderness does not remain at ideal levels and culling drastically erodes these levels. Choosing and eradicating an entire breeding herd at random is an act of unselective genetic depletion. It induces the remaining genetically depleted population to respond by breeding at more regular intervals to replace their losses. A vicious cycle soon becomes established.

The alternative is to adopt a laissez-faire policy in which the elephants alter the habitat and in consequence regulate their own population. This policy was followed at Tsavo in Kenya, and despite the predictions of the 'hands-on' advocates, disaster did not occur and severe drought did not wipe out the elephants or the black rhino. The resultant diversification of vegetation was of benefit to browser, grazer, predator, tourist and the country's foreign currency earnings. Recent research by soil scientists, hydrologists, botanists and zoologists indicates that a natural, cyclic environment regulated by the elephants had been put back in motion.

These magnificent animals, which create so much controversy today, evolved from a small hippopotamus-like ancestor nearly 50 million years ago. With the demise of the dinosaurs some 65 million years ago, mammals started to rule the world. Climatic and geological forces created change, causing new ecological relationships between vegetation, herbivores and predators. No longer was it necessary to remain small and furtive, as in the days of the 'terrible lizards'. In fact for the herbivore increase in size meant the ability to range further afield and take advantage of more food sources at different levels, as well as a defence against predation.

Mammals of the order *Proboscidea* took an evolutionary path that led to the development of a massive body supported by stout legs. Large heads on short necks left a relatively inflexible body which resulted in the gradual evolutionary development of a trunk, the wonder organ providing the necessary flexibility the torso lacked. The basic model was tried out in various configurations many times; the Deinotherium of 35 million years ago was about the size of today's elephant with a trunk of similar proportions, with tusks sprouting from the lower jaw. This version died out across its range of Eurasia and Africa about five million years ago, but was superseded by Primelephas. Primelephas was the progenitor of today's African and Asiatic elephants as well as the recently extinct cold-climate mammoths, which were hunted to extinction by early hunters during the last Ice Age, some 10 000 years ago. As early as 40 000 years ago, our cave-dwelling ancestors were carving mammoth ivory into fertility charms and trinkets — a custom that was to be handed down through generations.

Geological change takes place slowly and the African continent has been relatively stable over the past two million years. Prim-

elephas would have roamed over a landscape similar to the Africa of just a century ago.

Social structure

Today's African elephant (*Loxodonta africana*), with the forest elephant subspecies (*Loxodonta africana cyclotis*) of the equatorial forests, lives in a well-structured, stable matriarchal family unit. This family unit gains experience and knowledge from generation to generation. The combined memory bank of the matriarchs imparts the necessary learning skills to the young to ensure survival in the harsh African bush. Knowledge is passed from mother to young on how to behave and

tain close ties with the original. Males, on reaching puberty at about 14 years, are driven from the herd to form loosely associated bachelor herds. Though the comings and goings of the males are more random, their communications keep them in constant touch with other family units.

The stages of an elephant's life closely mirror those of man, and cover a similar time span. Infancy, childhood, puberty, parenthood and old age coincide remarkably with those of humans. As in the case of humans, most knowledge is accumulated in childhood. Elephants have a highly developed brain enabling them to store, group and retain individual memories.

Below left: *A bird's-eye view of an elephant offered by the hide at Big Toms Pan shows the back length, a useful technique for assessing elephant age.*
Below: *A fine specimen of a mature bull elephant, encrusted in mud and dust, who has lived his 50-odd years in the relative security of Hwange National Park.*

where to get certain foods and water in times of plenty as well as in times of hardship.

Social bonding within the family group is strong. Members of a family unit help each other in times of stress and rearing of youngsters is a group responsibility; lactating females often suckle the young of others. The family unit comprises mothers and daughters of various ages and prepubescent males. Daughters invariably remain with the family unit all their lives, but if it becomes too large they may form their own family unit which will main-

Age

Estimating the age of elephants in the field has been done using several methods of varying levels of technicality. Infants of up to one year can walk beneath their mother's belly and tusks only become visible in juveniles of about two years of age, whilst intermediates about six years old are roughly half the height of an adult cow. Harvey Croze developed a method of photographing elephant from the air and measuring their back lengths, a remarkably reliable field technique of estimating age.

The correlation of increase in age and size and the growth of tusk size also helps with estimation of age in the field. After eruption at about two years of age, tusks grow continuously throughout life. Transposed onto a graph, female tusk growth is normally a straight line. The tusk weighs about 3 kg at puberty and grows to 18 kg by the end of their lifespan. Bulls do not exhibit such a general trend and size can vary tremendously. Whilst female tusks tend to be long and slender, those of bulls tend to thicken as they grow, which also helps to determine the sex of elephants in the field. Estimation of tusk size is hampered by wear and tear of tusks and

Below: The elephant pecking order is clearly evident as a queue forms to drink from the borehole outlet at Big Toms Pan.

Tooth	Age in years
M1	1
M2	2
M3	6
M4	15
M5	28
M6	47

Above: *An elephant's age can be estimated by the study of its molars.*

many elephants break off tusks during their lives, especially in Hwange where they do a lot of digging for salts and gouging tree trunks to peel off bark. Tuskless females are far more common than tuskless bulls.

Once again post mortem work provides us with more detailed information about elephant society and age structure. In 1969 Lawes, Parker and Archer confirmed that the dimensions of the dissected hind leg bone bore a close relationship to the owner's total body mass. Now that the relationship has been established for both sexes, the dissected hind leg can be used to predict the total body mass and hence the age quite accurately, so it is now a widely used technique.

The most commonly used aging technique applied to dead elephants is the study of their teeth, or rather their molars, as their tusks are specially adapted incisors. Six molars develop on each side of the upper and lower jaw of the elephant's mouth cavity, all of which are deciduous or shed during the elephant's life. At no time are more than two of these molars in wear simultaneously in any one half of the jaw. Small fragments get worn down and are broken off and the next molar grows forward from the back of the jaw to replace it. The molars are designated M1 through to M6 and Laws concluded that they were fully developed and erupted, but not worn down, at the ages shown in the table on page 37.

Not only does tooth configuration confirm animal age reasonably accurately, but the wear rate affects the elephant's longevity. Wear rates vary considerably according to the environment and vegetation; what the elephant eats controls its eventual lifespan. The coarser the food, the greater the wear rate of the molars and the sooner they are replaced. As the final molar M6 wears down, it places an upper limit on the elephant of around 60 years of age. Elephant dung with large undigested fibres is from old elephants with well worn M6 molars who do not have long to live. Only very occasionally do elephants have a supernumerary molar, or M7, which may add a few more years to their life.

Sexuality

As elephants mature and the difference between male and female becomes more apparent, a feature known as sexual dimorphism becomes evident. This is a useful way of telling the sexes apart and concerns the shape of the forehead. In females it has a peaked appearance in profile; in males it curves smoothly forward and downwards. Group composition also gives a clue to the animal's sex and age. All members of a bachelor group will be post-pubertal males and the absence of young elephants is obvious. Solitary individuals are invariably males, whilst only mature bulls associate with breeding herds since young bulls of 15 years or so are evicted from

Below: *Hwange's bulls are among the largest in Africa. Here three magnificent bulls show their size and bulk.*

the herd on reaching puberty. These adolescent males are often solitary or occur in smaller bachelor groups. As they still have a lot of growing to do, their shoulder size is not an indication of sex, nor have they yet developed the domed forehead so diagnostic of an adult bull. Usually the best way to identify their gender is by the broader circumference of the base of the tusks.

The most common way of determining an animal's sex, examining the external genitalia, is not straightforward in the elephant. Males have no scrotum and the testes are situated inside the body cavity close to the kidneys. Mammals with a scrotum are able to keep the testes below normal body temperature and spermatozoa are stored in a distinct epididymis on top of each of the testes. Having the testes within the body cavity, which has an average body temperature of 37 °C, means that in the elephant the process of spermatozoa production is not temperature-sensitive. Furthermore, an elephant's testes have no epididymis, but rather a long duct to the seminal vesicle which performs the function of the epididymis, i.e. storage, concentration and

maturation of the spermatozoa.

Normally the penis is retracted and sheathed within the body cavity and is not always evident to assist in confirming gender. One means of counting elephants at waterholes during a game count, when they are concentrated in a large mass, is to count the number of legs and divide by four. Should an adult bull be in the mass and feeling rather relaxed, his 'fifth' leg can give rise to some complicated mathematics and some odd results!

Because the vagina of the female is ventrally situated, successful mating requires the male to have a proportionately long and unusually shaped penis. Special levator muscles account for the characteristic 'S' shape of the erect penis which enables the male to hook the tip of the penis into the vagina. As only about 60 cm of the penis enters the vagina no less than 1 litre of ejaculate is required to ensure enough spermatozoa reach the uterus to bring about fertilisation.

The phenomenon of *musth* was not generally thought to occur in African elephants as it does in Asiatic elephants, and was only confirmed some 15 years ago. Musth is a time when the males become more aggressive owing to high testosterone levels. The condition of musth manifests itself in the form of a copious secretion from a temporal gland and frequent discharges of urine. Musth usually afflicts males of 30 and upwards and these

musth bulls tend to associate more with the breed herds. Musth tends to be more common in the rainy season, which also corresponds with a peak in the oestrus activity of many females, though breeding can occur at any time during the year.

When several musth bulls contest the right to mate with a cow in season, a test for dominance can ensue. Dominance may be established from prior contact, but if not, a fight follows. Fights are normally pushing and shoving matches with a lot of shrill vocalising. They seldom get serious, but if the adversaries are evenly matched the bout can hot up and tusks may be brought into action. Serious injury is not common, but bulls are occasionally killed while fighting, more often by accident than intent.

When a cow comes into oestrus she may mate with several bulls, but usually the most dominant bull will establish his right to mate, especially if he is in musth. He will accompany the female diligently, mating frequently to increase the chance of passing on his genes. Mating is a surprisingly gentle act for such a colossal beast. The male, who is constantly in attendance, pacifies the female by stroking her back with his trunk and giving off low, resonant rumbles. When the female gives in to his advances, the male mounts her with his forelegs straddling her back, whilst the trunk continues to caress her head and back, giving more reassurance. Copulation usually lasts for only about a minute and is accompanied by more loud grumbling sounds. The act often causes great excitement within the rest of the breed herd. The length of the oestrus cycle in the African elephant was found by researcher Cynthia Moss in Amboseli to be about three weeks, as with the Asiatic elephant. Post mortems show that an ovary ovulates several times during the oestrus cycle and more than one ovulation is required to ensure pregnancy.

Few people have been lucky enough to witness the birth of an African elephant in the wild. At parturition the female walks backwards and bends her hind legs, taking up a squatting posture. Birth is usually quick and causes great excitement within the herd. All members are keen to inspect the new arrival, sniffing it with outstretched trunks since etiquette prevents them from crowding the mother and youngster. Often the matriarch is the only member of the herd allowed up close at first. The mother seems intent on peeling off the foetal membranes and assisting the newborn infant to its feet, gently lifting it with trunk and forefeet as quickly as possible. She will invariably eat some of the placenta, a practice common in many animals as the hormones in the placenta stimulate milk production. Often the infant is on its feet within 20 minutes and trying to suckle soon after. As the breasts are situated between the front legs, the mother patiently guides the infant to them if it spends too much time blundering around the wrong end! The youngster lifts its trunk up and back slightly to one side and suckles with its mouth. Suckling will continue for the next two years when the youngster is normally weaned, or longer if the calving period is extended to five or six years.

Below: A bull in musth, identified by the obvious discharge from his temporal gland. Musth can occur at any time of the year, but is more noticeable during the rains when the females come into season.

Top: *A cow pauses after drinking to allow her calf to suckle peacefully.* Above: *A family of elephants dig salts from the licks around Konondo Pan.*

Death and disease

Mortality within an elephant population is obviously an important factor when considering their demographics. Predation is relatively rare though many predators and scavengers feed off elephants that have succumbed to other causes. Young calves that are separated from their mothers or orphaned at an early age are obviously prone to predation by lion and hyena, but normally elephants go in fear of no one except man.

Parasites are found in all wild elephants and Dr John Condy, former director of Zimbabwe's Department of National Parks and Wild Life Services, did a comprehensive survey of parasitism in Hwange's elephant population. He detailed ten genera of internal parasites and concluded that levels of parasite contamination should be monitored as indicators of overpopulation. Parasites normally have a debilitating effect on the host in times

Right: *A female stands still to allow her large calf to suckle. Unlike most mammals, elephants have mamillary glands between their front legs.*

of stress, when they multiply beyond normal levels of contamination and have a detrimental effect on the host's general wellbeing. Dr Condy found that the water troughs on which so many of Hwange's animals depend are contaminated by faeces as they are at ground level. Such faecal contamination can cause unnatural buildups in infective nematode larvae, which are quickly transferred from sick to healthy animals. Dr Condy recommended that the lip of the troughs be raised a metre above ground level. This would greatly reduce faecal contamination but could cause problems for smaller animals wanting to drink from the troughs, which are the only source of water if the pans dry up.

Cardiovascular disease such as arteriosclerosis has been found in elephants. It is normally associated with aging but can also result from stresses such as drought, overpopulation, disrupted migratory habits and breeding patterns, poaching and culling.

Accidents obviously take their toll. One common cause of accidental death is being crushed by falling trees, often the result of the elephant's own feeding damage. This happens particularly in species such as the baobab. Snake bites and drowning account for individual deaths, mostly of juveniles, and falls from rocky places and following treacherous game trails also take their toll. Obviously the latter two hardly apply to Hwange as a noticeable form of mortality. One regular cause of death to Hwange's elephants is collision with trains as the main Bulawayo-Victoria Falls railway line forms part of the park's northwest boundary. Night-time collisions happen quite regularly and often park staff have to track down badly wounded casualties that were not killed outright, and put them out of their misery. Even the largest land mammal is no match for a 20th Class Garratt steam locomotive.

Drought is one of the major natural causes of mortality in African elephants. Not only does drought deprive the elephants of all essential water for drinking and bathing, but it also restricts plant growth and elephants can quickly lose condition if food resources are moribund and over-utilised. In such times of

Above: *A large bull chases off a buffalo that is desperate to drink. In drought years elephants monopolise pans, especially the outlet troughs, often at the expense of other thirsty animals.*
Above right: *One of the casualties of the water shortage.*
Right: *During drought baobabs may be toppled by the intensive feeding pressure of hungry elephants who eat the sinuous fibres, extracting much-needed moisture and minerals.*
Below right: *A matriarch stands over her daughter who was darted by rangers to remove a heavy-duty snare from around her neck.*

stress when the animal is nutritionally impoverished, parasitic contamination, disease and psychological disturbance all stand to compound its misery.

In Hwange all these mortality factors have an influence on the population from time to time in varying degrees, but the main cause of natural population control is aging. The aged gradually starve to death as their teeth wear down and they are unable to grind their food enough to allow adequate digestion. In the face of plenty the old die of lack of food, having as it were dug their own graves with their teeth.

It is said that an elephant never forgets, and this may be closer to the mark than originally appreciated. The reaction of living elephants to the remains of dead elephants is startling and sometimes very poignant. A herd will often sniff the remains reverently while standing silently as if holding two minutes' silence. When the herd moves on, an individual will occasionally remain and continue to fondle a particular bone, sometimes carrying this object around for some time. Elephants have often been observed trying to bury such remains. In the course of her research in Tsavo, Cynthia Moss documented cases of elephants removing the tusks of dead, poached elephants whose ivory had not yet been recovered by the poachers, carrying them away and in some cases smashing them on rocks. Are elephants capable of deducing that humans kill them for their tusks? This is an interesting notion and one that cannot be dismissed out of hand until we learn more about the elephant.

For the present elephants seem to be secure at Hwange. Scenes of peaceful contentment and family bliss await the tourist lucky enough to visit the park. Gatherings of up to 100 elephants are commonplace at the main watering holes during the dry season, providing visitors with a chance to watch, study and enjoy these magnificent leviathans of the African bush.

CHAPTER 6

HWANGE'S OTHER ANIMALS

*'To see 10 000 animals untamed and not branded
with the symbols of human commerce is like scaling an
unconquered mountain for the first time, or like finding a forest
without roads or footpaths or the blemish of an axe.'*

Beryl Markham

Though the elephant is one of Hwange's main attractions, the park has a bewildering variety of fauna. Many other species of animals, both large and small, abound — some in spectacular concentrations at certain times of the year. The highly diverse nature of the bushveld allows for a great variety of species, and it is a much more productive regime than one devoted to domestic livestock husbandry. This level of utilisation is also self-sustaining, as nature does not allow the natural inhabitants to get away with destructive feeding habits such as those of cattle, sheep or other domestic livestock. The bush supports an intricate web of life with vegetation playing the pivotal role in the chain. Large primary users play an obvious part, whether grazers or browsers, but highly varied forms of life act as secondary users. These range from birds and reptiles through to insects, parasitic plants, fungi, lichen and even the humble bacteria. All have their role in maintaining a stable, self-sustaining cycle.

Left: *A male lion yawns in the early morning after a long night spent walking to Ngweshla Pan.*
Above: *A group of wildebeest canter past. These strange-looking antelope are common in the grasslands near Main Camp.*

Predators

Predators play an essential role in this web of life, helping to control the numbers of prey species. This in turn regulates the rate of increase of the predators, finely balancing the populations of both groups. Hwange contains most of Africa's large predators and many of the small ones. Mention the word 'predator' in Africa and most people automatically think of lion. Hwange has its fair share, but many visitors are disappointed when they do not see them. The king of the beasts is, by nature, indolent, spending as much as 20 out of 24 hours resting, usually in thick cover. This stacks the odds against bumping into him. The lions' few hours of activity are invariably at night, since the concealment offered by darkness greatly increases the chance of a successful hunt. Hwange's lions seem to be predominantly nocturnal, a habit probably enforced by the eradication programme in the park's early days when the lions who were more active by day were eliminated. However, when active lions can cover a distance of up to 20 km. As darkness falls the lions call, males proclaiming their territory and females mainly keeping in touch with their young and other pride members. Though the night often reverberates with their throaty roars, the eager visitor is frustrated by their disappearing act when first light comes and entrance gates open.

Lions are the only truly sociable members of the cat family and their lives are shaped around the pride. The females are the nucleus and are usually related. They are the stable element in the pride's composition and are normally members for life.

Young males are evicted from the pride at about two years of age and then lead a nomadic existence, often teaming up with their brothers and other dispossessed males to form small bachelor groups. These nomads bide their time and when fully mature will make a bid to oust other resident males from their prides. Single resident males stand little chance if two or more nomads contest their dominance. These territorial fights can be vicious and, at times, lethal to one or more protagonists, a major factor in the mortality rate of adult males. Should the dispossessed male survive, then he in turn resumes a nomadic existence. The more resident males in

the pride the greater their chance of maintaining control over it and passing on their genes — their investment in the future so that their offspring survive the turbulent juvenile years. When leadership of the pride changes, the new male(s) kill all their predecessor's young cubs and drive off any sub-adult males. As a result the females of the pride come in season within a few days and the ice is broken in an orgy of extended mating and familiarisation.

Lions kill a wide range of prey and their size and strength ensure that singly or as a pride they can hunt the largest of herbivores. Their phenomenal strength means they can literally poleaxe large antelope with one blow, but prey is normally killed by suffocation before or after immobilisation with a spinal bite by others in the pride. Death can be prolonged,

Above: *A young male leopard stretches languidly before starting to hunt.*
Right, from top to bottom: *A 2,4 m crocodile makes short work of an adult male vervet monkey who paid the ultimate price for lack of caution when drinking from a waterhole on Hwange Safari Lodge Estate.*

taking up to 20 minutes for large animals, but shock spares the victim most of the pain of literally being eaten alive. Lions do not always have things their own way as their favoured prey, the buffalo, make formidable adversaries. Lions tend to single out the weak, old or young buffalo in the panic of stampede rather than risk head-on confrontation. Giraffe are another favoured prey species and many bear scars on their hindquarters from attacks where a lion has tried to trip them up and make them stumble where they are most vulnerable. Their massive hooves can be a well-aimed weapon, however. Zebra can also lash out with vicious kicks whilst in full flight and inflict serious wounds, so the lions certainly do not have an easy time of hunting. In hard times they will resort to rodents and birds and gain moisture from gemsbok cucumbers.

The other big cats of Hwange are the leopard and cheetah, the spotted hunters. Leopards are solitary and secretive and though not often seen are widespread throughout the region and relatively common in the park. Predominantly nocturnal, they are extremely powerful hunters of small antelope, game birds, rodents and even fish. They rely on stealth and concealment to get them as close as possible to the prey, then end the hunt in an explosive burst of speed as the prey is pulled down. If the prey animal is large enough, the leopard suffocates it in the same way as the lion suffocates its prey. The strength of the leopard can be gauged by its ability to haul prey as large as bushbuck and impala up into the trees, which keeps it away from vultures and other scavengers — except for the honey badger, which usurps at will!

Cheetah, on the other hand, are diurnal, hunting by day and relying on their incredible speed, combined with a preliminary stalk, to run down their prey. They are mainly hunters of smaller antelope such as impala and reedbuck. They also hunt warthog, ostrich and smaller prey such as hares, and they kill by strangulation. The cheetah's hunting methods are more suited to open areas than to Hwange's predominantly woodland and scrub zones, so the park's complement of cheetahs is low — about 150 animals at present.

Another important predatory role is fulfilled by the spotted hyena, again a highly social and nocturnal hunter. Closely knit clans, dominated by the matriarchs, are efficient and well synchronised hunters, capable of running

Below: *Hwange is one of the last bastions of the African wild dog – the reserve's growing population of the 'painted wolves' is estimated at 340 animals.*

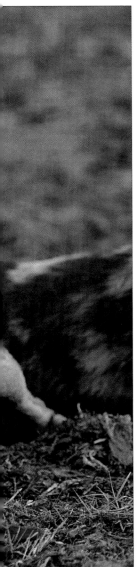

Right: *A white or square-lipped rhino, so called because of a corruption of the Dutch word 'wyd' meaning 'wide' and referring to the lip structure evolved for cropping and grazing.*

down prey over long distances. Cooperation allows them to pull down zebra, kudu and wildebeest, prey too large for an individual to cope with. They are not the skulking cowards originally portrayed, though they still rely heavily on scavenging on the prey remains of other predators and their legendary jaws can crunch up bones as tough as a buffalo's thighbone. Their success as hunters is shown by the fact that lions often scavenge hyena kills. The brown hyena is very occasionally sighted in Hwange, which is the fringe of its range as the animal prefers the dry Kalahari proper.

Smaller predatory cats such as serval and caracal are also seldom seen because of their solitary nocturnal natures, but they are highly efficient predators of rodents, birds and reptiles. More commonly seen are the various species of mongoose. Groups of banded and dwarf mongoose are fascinating to watch as they scurry around foraging for a wide variety of food, but one or two are always on sentry duty making sure that they, in turn, do not become the hunted.

Many of Hwange's predators are highly specialised feeders. These include the bateared fox with its huge ears and acute hearing, which helps it locate grubs and larvae by their subterranean rustlings and scratchings. The bateared fox will pinpoint its prey with unerring accuracy, dig them up and bolt them down. The aardwolf is extremely specialised even to its rudimentary dentition, relying exclusively on a diet of termites and harvester ants, diametrically opposed in habit to the cosmopolitan jackal, sidestriped and blackbacked, both being found in Hwange. The blackbacked jackal is by far the more common of the two and is the nocturnal songster of the African bush.

The African wild dog is one of the world's most endangered predators and Hwange one of its last bastions. Extensive research started by Dr Joshua Ginsburg and continued by local researcher Greg Rasmussen is helping to unravel many of the complexities of the wild dog's way of life — essential to save these magnificent canines from the dark abyss of extinction. Living in well-regulated and highly social packs under the patronage of a dominant pair, they exhibit many of the finer qualities that human society aspires to, such as communal care of the young, old and sick. Vigorously hunted by man nearly to extinction because of their hunting abilities, the remnant populations are still under threat, even in the sanctity of Hwange. Common canine ailments such as rabies and distemper take their toll. Because these wide-ranging dogs need vast areas to roam, they are in constant threat of being shot on sight by unsympathetic farmers, but attitudes are slowly changing. A few dogs are run over and killed each year on the main roads, a loss the species can ill afford. To help cut down this toll, road signs have been put up at major crossings warning motorists of possible wild dog presence and to reduce speed. Latest figures show that the 'painted wolves' of Hwange are holding their own and even increasing in numbers, a most encouraging trend for the future.

Rhino

Other endangered inhabitants are the black and white rhinos. Recent and unrelenting poaching has virtually decimated the park's rhino population, a major setback in their conservation. The white rhino was hunted to extinction in Zimbabwe by the early white hunters and settlers, but was reintroduced with stock imported from Natal in 1966. Black rhino hung on in the remote hilly areas near Sinamatella and their numbers were bolstered by the introduction of 40 animals between 1963 and 1965. Refugees from the

flooding of Lake Kariba during Operation Noah, together with the white rhino, started to breed well and formed sound, healthy populations until they were callously gunned down for their horns. The price of the rhino horn is on the increase and this may prove to be the death knell for the dwindling rhino population.

Antelopes

Other rare and vulnerable inhabitants of Hwange are the magnificent sable and roan antelopes, closely related members of the genus *Hippotragus*. Second largest of all the antelope, the roan is a highly selective grazer which self-limits its range to the more open grassland areas. The slightly smaller sable is probably the most magnificent member of the antelope family. The males have a jet black coat, offset by striking white facial markings and sweeping curved horns. The females have a browner coat and their horns are less curved, but they are particularly good at using them to ward off predators, even lions, when protecting their young.

Eland are common in the more open

Above: *The rich hues of these impala are accentuated by the soft light of the afternoon.*
Right: *Juvenile baboons at rest.*

Wildebeest are common in the open grassland around the Main Camp and Makololo areas. In the early years of the park's existence Ted Davidson, the first warden, reported large-scale migrations of wildebeest crossing the swollen Sibanini River in the far south of the park. It is hard to imagine this in these drier times. These herds were part of the vast population of the Kalahari whose migrations once rivalled those of the Serengeti, but are now, sadly, a thing of the past. A border fence along the boundary with Botswana halted the seasonal migrations to the Makgadikgadi Pans and today's wildebeest are a static remnant population of these Kalahari nomads.

The bushbuck was not originally recorded within the boundaries of Hwange in the early days, but by 1940 several of these small, secretive antelope were resident at Inyantue Dam. Their favoured habitat is riverine woodlands and these new immigrants were obviously colonising suitable habitat in the park along the watercourses. Today bushbuck are found around Bumbusi, Sinamatella, Inyantue and through the Hwange Safari Lodge Estate, past Main Camp and as far into the park as Makwa Pan. Although widespread, they are not common. The deep red-brown coat, marked with white spots and stripes, makes this animal particularly striking and very well camouflaged in the dappled light of riparian growth.

Primates

A symbiotic relationship exists between the bushbuck and the chacma baboon. Bushbuck are often seen feeding on the debris dropped by a troop of baboons feeding in the tree canopies, each gaining added security from the vigilance of the other. Large baboon troops, up to 50 strong, are often encountered in the park and their antics are a source of constant amusement. Their rigorous social hierarchy is easy to work out and only the young seem to get away

woodland areas of the park and at calving time during the rainy season they congregate in huge herds of several hundred animals. Largest of all the antelopes, a mature bull can weigh up to 750 kg and looks remarkably bovine with a heavy dewlap. Despite their bulk, they are very agile and capable of jumping and clearing most fences. The males tend to live a rather solitary existence. A strange clicking sound, often heard in the still of a winter's night, is made by a bull eland as the halves of his front hooves click together with each step he takes.

with lapses in etiquette. Newborn infants cling to their mothers' bellies, pink-faced and pink-eared, and they are jealously guarded by their mothers from other inquisitive females. As they grow and become more precocious, they ride on their mothers' backs jockey style and form vigorous play groups aimed at developing agility and laying the foundations for later status within the troop. Dominant males lead the group's daily activities, taking turns at sentry duties. As the troop forages for food clashes are frequent, highly vocal and sometimes aggressive, especially when males contest their position in the pecking order.

The park's other primates, the vervet monkeys, occur in smaller family groups of up to 20 individuals. Omnivorous, like the baboon, the vervet has a distinct range of vocalisation and research in East Africa has documented over 30 distinct calls each with a specific meaning. All members of the troop react appropriately to the cry, whether it is a call for vigilance or warning of imminent danger.

Other mammals

The largest concentrations of any of the park's mammal inhabitants are undoubtedly the dry-season accumulations of buffalo. Herds of over 2 000 animals can aggregate by the end of the dry season, constantly on the move in search of dwindling pasture. Herds of this size have an enormous impact on the vegetation, leaving behind huge swathes of trampled grass. As the waterholes dry up these huge herds can demolish small pans, churning them up into seas of useless mud. The progress of the herds can be followed by enormous clouds of dust which they raise — often visible an hour or more before the herd can be seen making its way to the waterhole. Lions often follow these vast herds, assured of a constant supply of

Above: *A family group of zebra — dominant stallion, mares and their offspring in the late afternoon.*

food. With the onset of the rains the herds break up into smaller herds of several hundred buffalo, as the urge to be always on the move is tempered by the abundance of grazing and water.

Hippopotamuses may seem to be unlikely inhabitants of the Kalahari — an area devoid of reliable water. Several of the larger pans and dams, such as Makololo and Mandavu, have resident groups but nomad vagrants can pitch up in the strangest of places for a few days before moving on. Some semi-nomadic hippos have a series of pans they visit, as though on a regular roster. Weighing up to 1 500 kg, the males are highly territorial and in the restricted environment of a pan they are all very aggressive. Often females with small young will move off to other pans to prevent their babies, particularly the young bulls, being killed. The increase in the numbers of hippo is no doubt due in part to increased human pressure along the Gwayi River, which has forced the hippo into more marginal areas free from persecution.

Warthog are common in most areas of the park where there is reliable water. They are regular visitors to pans and though not totally dependant on surface water, they revel in mud wallows. These ungainly creatures shuffle around on their front knees whilst eating uprooted grass rhizomes as well as cropping grass. They are constantly grunting, keeping in contact with all members of the family group. When startled, they run off with surprising speed with tails held high. Whilst the warthog is diurnal and sleeps at night in old aardvark holes, its cousin, the larger boar-like bushpig, is nocturnal. Lacking the huge facial warts and large incisor tusks of the warthog, these reddish-brown pigs have a just reputation for being aggressive and make formidable adversaries with their small, razor-sharp tusks.

One of the strangest and most rarely seen animals of Hwange is the pangolin. The armour plating of specially adapted matted hair makes the pangolin seem like a remnant from the time of the dinosaurs. The animal walks around on its hind legs using its long,

Below left: *The South African hedgehog, listed as rare in the IUCN Red Data List, is normally nocturnal but is often active during the day after rain.* Below right: *A large group of banded mongooses stare inquisitively from the safety of an old termite mound, one of the boltholes in their territory.* Bottom left: *An impressive buffalo bull, often referred to as a 'dagga boy'.* Bottom right: *A rare sight — the elusive nocturnal scaly anteater, or pangolin.*

heavy tail as a counterbalance, so that the heavily clawed front legs are free to rip open ant and termite nests. The pangolin has a very long, sticky tongue with which it laps up ants deep within the nest's tunnels. To protect itself from predators, especially its vulnerable underparts, the pangolin rolls itself into a tight ball, curling its tail over its head. The single young, born during the winter, is carried around clinging to its mother's tail. If threatened the mother curls up, protecting the infant within the armour-plated ball.

Hwange is inhabited by a large number of rodents ranging in size from Africa's largest — the prickly porcupine — to one of the world's smallest mammals, the diminutive pygmy mouse. The porcupine, like most rodents, is nocturnal and wanders far and wide in search of bulbs, tubers and roots as well as fruit, bark and, on occasion, even carrion. One unusual trait is its habit of gnawing on the ivory of dead elephants. This is probably to provide the rodent with minerals, especially calcium, and to help prune its constantly growing incisors. When disturbed, the porcupine freezes and if it feels threatened, it becomes aggressive, stamping its back feet, grunting and rattling its tail quills. This is the final warning which all are well advised to heed. Many a predator and unwary person has felt the painful stab of quills as they embed in the flesh as a consequence of the porcupine's sudden, backward rush. These wounds can quickly become septic and have led to a miserable death for many an old or sick lion trying to get a quick, but certainly not easy, meal. Whereas the porcupine tips the scales at about 18 kg, the pygmy mouse weighs only 5 g and has a total body/tail length of 10 cm. They excavate their own tiny burrows, and furtively scurry about at night, searching for grass seeds, greenery and insects.

The creatures of the night are many and varied, the strangest being the springhare, somewhat akin to a giant gerbil. Springhares live in loosely associated communities in excavated burrows and many a tourist has shaken his head in disbelief on sighting this strange creature, which hops around like a small kangaroo. The antbear, or aardvark, is one of nature's oddities, weighing up to 65 kg and measuring about 1,6 m in length. Its appearance is best described as pig-like, but with a long muzzle, long tubular ears and a thick, tapering tail. Armed with huge powerful claws, with which they excavate extensive tunnels scattered around their large territories, aardvarks are the homemakers for many other species who readily usurp these tunnels. Their claws can rip into termite mounds with ease and they feed exclusively on termites, which they also lap up with a long, sticky tongue. Their armament of strong, sharp claws also acts as an effective deterrent to predators.

The lesser bushbaby is a highly active arboreal acrobat. Its huge forward-directed eyes show up as bright yellow-red glowing coals in the light of a vehicle's headlights, disappearing in a flash as it bounds off. Also specialised feeders, these family groups leap and bound around the trees in search of gums and resins. They augment this unusual diet with insects which they grab with unerring accuracy with their hands.

The diversity of life is greater in Hwange than in any other national park in Zimbabwe. It ranges from the giraffe, the world's tallest mammal with the unique ability of being able to clean its ears with its tongue, to the subterranean molerat which lives its entire life underground and is able to carry on its business hidden from the view of all.

Right: *Regal waterbuck rams at Kanondo Pan.* Below: *A pair of tree squirrels bask in the early morning sun at the entrance to their drey.*

HWANGE'S BIRDS

'Will the sky above Africa indeed become the blue stone where no vultures fly? We wish with all our hearts that many future generations will enjoy and cherish the sight of the big birds riding the high winds.'

Ian Player

To the ornithologist, the birdlife of Hwange is a cornucopia, a never-ending feast. Over 400 species have been recorded to date and as time goes by more are added to the list. Special birdwatching safaris cater for the keen ornithologist hoping to add to his personal tally, or even spot a species that hasn't been observed in the area before.

The various diverse vegetational zones provide ideal habitats for specialised feeders and to do justice to an ornithological safari a stay at each of the camps is recommended.

The transition in tree and plant zones brings about a change in the distribution of closely related species. Two good examples of this belong to the hornbill family, the disproportionately beaked *kolokolo* bird of Rudyard Kipling's banks of the 'grey-green, greasy Limpopo'. The grey Bradfield's hornbill is closely associated with stands of teak trees and is common around Main Camp, whilst at Sinamatella the slightly darker but very similar crowned hornbill replaces it in the mopane woodlands. Similarly, the yellowbilled hornbill is an inhabitant of the thornveld while its cousin the redbilled

Left: *The yellowbilled hornbill is a common resident of the park's stands of thorn trees and mixed scrub.* Above: *A lanner falcon feeding on flying ants in mid-flight.*

hornbill is also closely associated with mopane woodland. Slightly different environmental needs have evolved to separate such similar-looking birds geographically. The grey hornbill, on the other hand, is found throughout the park, being far less demanding in its requirements. The largest member of the family, the ground hornbill with its sonorous, booming call, is similarly wide ranging.

The hornbills all have a similar breeding biology — one of the most unusual in the bird world. They nest in holes in trees, which they line with grass, leaves, or bark chips. The female enters the nest hole to lay the eggs and incubate them. In a unique behavioural trait, the male will seal up the nest entrance with mud cemented by crushed insects, entombing his partner in the nest. He leaves only a narrow slit open, to allow the female to breathe

for the duration of the incubation and most of the fledging period. The hornbills' distinctive large beaks are probably an adaptation for this behaviour, making it easy to pass food through the narrow slit. When the female starts to incubate she simultaneously moults her wing and tail feathers, obviously to avoid fouling her plumage in the cramped space. Now she is totally dependent on the male for sustenance for the 45 to 50 days she remains in the nest.

During this period the male is constantly foraging for food, a necessity which probably accounts for the high level of variety in hornbill diets. True omnivores, hornbills eat just about anything ranging through insects, scorpions, solifugids, centipedes, caterpillars, lizards, rodents, seeds, fruit, eggs and even nestlings. When the young hatch, the male's

Above: *A whitebacked vulture takes on the texture of the tree in which it roosts in the fading light of a winter afternoon.*

already busy schedule becomes even more hectic, with an extra three to five ravenous mouths to feed. The female breaks free of the nest about 24 days after the first egg hatches and at long last the overworked male gets some help feeding the hungry beaks behind the slit entrance. When the female breaks out of the nest cavity, the youngsters instinctively patch up the break and restore the narrow feeding slit, using droppings, food and nest debris. The narrow entrance provides protection by acting as a barrier and preventing most predators from forcing their way into the nest. As the young leave the nest one by one a day or two apart, in accordance with the sequence of egg laying and hatching, the remaining chicks continue to rebuild the entrance until the last one leaves. Even with the young fledged, the hardworking parents have to feed their young until they have learnt what is edible by observation, trial and error. Parental care is taken to the extreme by the ground hornbill, which will feed its offspring for up to 12 months when they are large and have long left the nest — unusual in the avian world!

Another nester in tree holes is the oxpecker, of which both species are found in Hwange and are a common sight as they perch on their favoured hosts. Both redbilled and yellowbilled oxpeckers associate with buffalo, rhino, eland, kudu, impala, sable, zebra, warthog and hippo, but their favourite host is the giraffe. They clamber around their hosts, usually benefiting them by removing ticks, horseflies and ectoparasitic invertebrates. Their annoying habit of picking at scar tissue and open wounds gets tedious and irritating and, at times, painful to the host who will attempt, usually in vain, to dislodge them. The distinctive crackling, hissing call of this bird is a sound of the bush that one is well advised to take heed of and, if on foot, proceed with caution — they not only give early warning to hikers, but to the host as well.

Visitors to Hwange are enthralled by the iridescent colours of so many of the birds, which dazzle the eye and relieve the monotony of the drab winter bushveld. Among the most colourful are the lilacbreasted rollers with their brilliant azure wing feathers, the beautiful

Above right: *Common to the open grassy areas of the park, the capped wheatear is a very active little bird, always on the move.*
Right: *The male redheaded finch is similar in size, appearance and habits to the cutthroat finch, but is easier to identify.*

golden oriole, the blue-eared glossy starling with its metallic sheen, and the diminutive sunbirds and tiny malachite kingfisher.

Whilst colour constantly attracts the attention, the ear is often baffled by a cacophony of song. The melodies of Heuglin's robin are judged the finest of the African songbirds and the sounds of melodic tunes are often the only clue to myriad species lurking in thick scrub or high in the tree canopy. The ability to identify song is often the only sure way of identifying species. The plethora of small brown larks, cisticolas, warblers, and prinias — known colloquially to birders as 'little brown jobs' (LBJs), can be virtually impossible to identify visually even with the best binoculars. In some species visual identification can only be confirmed by a couple of grams difference in body weight, colours on the inside of the gape (or mouth) or soles of feet and even the position of indents on primary wing feathers, which can all prove very frustrating.

However, a tape recording of bird calls can prove beyond a doubt the identity of an infuriating LBJ lurking in the grass. Just play the call of various species in the same family and when you play the relevant one, you are guaranteed an immediate response, sometimes even triggering off a frantic territorial display. One more species to tick off the list!

Hwange is particularly rich in raptors and though most of the large eagles and vultures are easy to recognise, many of the small accipiters, goshawks and sparrowhawks are hard to identify and even to spot in the first place. Being ambushers by nature, they still-hunt from concealed perches in trees and shrubs, waiting to single out suitable quarry, and then burst forth in a blur of speed. More evident in their hunting techniques, lanner falcons are common in the park and often seen making spectacular swoops over waterholes when hundreds of doves congregate to drink in the mornings and late afternoons.

Below: *A male knob-billed duck with the characteristic large fleshy carbuncle on its beak that signifies its readiness to pair off and mate.*

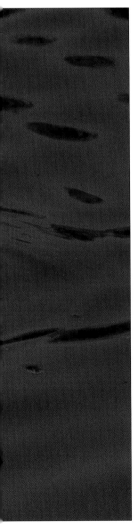

Right: A barred owl — one of the small hunters of the night.
Far right: Diminutive but spectacularly coloured, a pair of male violet-cheeked waxbills, common throughout Hwange, prepare to roost.

One of the most obvious and stylish of Hwange's raptors is the distinctive bateleur eagle, now becoming rare in areas where human pressure is growing, but holding its own in wilderness areas. The name derives from the French word for 'tumbler', which is a succinct description of the male during his display flights. The bateleur drifts aloft for hours on end in constant search of food, using thermals to maintain a constant speed of 60–80 km/h with the minimum of effort. The bateleur has a catholic diet, pouncing on birds, small mammals, reptiles, eggs, crabs and insects. It often pirates the kill of other large raptors, but is not averse to partaking of carrion if the need arises.

Whilst some birds are solitary others prefer the security of the flock; noisy gaggles of arrowmarked babblers, Meyer's parrots and redbilled hoopoe leave no doubt as to their presence and their raucous crescendos can disturb the soundest siesta. Of the communal birds, the gatherings of the redbilled quelea are the most awe inspiring. Quelea swarm in flocks of hundreds of thousands in good years. Although they weigh only a few grams each, their combined mass is so great that they can bring down the trees they roost in. They breed in massive colonies spread over several hectares. The communal noise of countless small chirps mounts into a deafening din, attracting every imaginable predator to feast on the windfall. Losses are immense, but a drop in the ocean in terms of the colony's numbers. The sheer volume of these huge flocks is best appreciated when they descend on a waterhole. The roar of countless tiny wingbeats is deafening as the flock rolls down to the water's edge to drink. As ever, the predators follow, but only the stragglers on the edges are picked off because any hawk foolhardy enough to fly into this maelstrom risks permanent injury!

Hwange also has many spectacularly large bird species. Kori bustards, the world's heaviest flying birds, stroll the grassy vleis in constant search of nourishment. The macabre marabou storks stand hunched beside the waterholes looking quite disconsolate. The stately crowned cranes honk and flap in ritual courtship dances and the secretary bird strides purposefully through the veld, self-absorbed by its daily routine.

Largest of all, the ostrich wanders the bush in small family groups, constantly on the move in an endless search for food. Like the hornbill, the ostrich will eat virtually anything. In the breeding season the larger, black-feathered males make startling booming noises which sound like the roars of a distant lion.

These calls are coupled with an elaborate courtship dance involving complex ritualised wheeling, spinning and pirouetting. If his attempts are successful, the male can entice several females to lay their eggs in the 3 m-wide nest which he has scraped into the sand. Each female can lay up to eight eggs which the male and his permanent partner will incubate in turn. The well-camouflaged female usually sits on the eggs by day and the darker male by night. The other egg-laying females go off, taking no further part in the procedure.

Befitting the world's largest bird, the eggs are gigantic, weighing over a kilogram apiece and with contents equivalent to two dozen hen's eggs. The newly hatched young are buff with dark streaks and in addition to this excellent camouflage they freeze in a crouching position when alarmed and are very difficult to see. This is particularly useful since so many predators enjoy baby ostrich. The parents actively shepherd the young around in a tightly chaperoned pack. The precocious youngsters grow quickly and soon keep up with the adults, who can run at speeds of 50-60 km/h and are capable of outrunning most adversaries.

Whilst the ostrich scrapes a huge shallow bowl in the sand, other birds invest far more time and energy in providing a safe environment for their eggs, the incubating mother and the young chicks. The francolin and guineafowl place their scrapes in the protection of thick grass and dense scrub. These rudimentary nests are vulnerable to predators simply stumbling onto them, however. Other species, such as the kingfishers and bee-eaters, make life more difficult by digging burrows into streambeds. Barbets and woodpeckers carve out nest holes in suitable tree trunks and branches, and one of these vacated holes is quickly snapped up by others unable to chip away at such hard material. Nest building is a more specialised art form. Nests range in complexity from that of the laughing dove, which simply fashions a few twigs into the shape of a loose bowl, to those of the grey lourie, eagle and vulture, which make large, stable stick platforms. These large birds are long-lived and territorial so an investment in a sound, stable nest is a wise move.

Another species that invests a lot of time and energy in nest building is the hamerkop. Its nest is a huge, domed structure wedged in the

Top: During the rainy season pairs of crowned cranes are common around pans and swampy grasslands. When not breeding, they form large nomadic flocks. Centre: The large and boldly marked saddlebill stork, usually seen in pairs, is resident at some of the larger, more reliable pans. Bottom: Whitebacked vultures squabble over the pickings of a kudu kill left by hyenas. A hooded vulture waits in the wings for whatever is left.

Above: *A little bee-eater puts on a flamboyant show as it hawks insects from a favoured perch.*

fork of a large tree, usually close to water. These nest structures can weigh over half a ton and the bird adds to them each year. The nest chamber is inside the huge mass, providing safety and security, whilst the roof of the dome acts as a display area where these kleptomaniacs show off their latest pickings, be they bones, shells, twigs or litter tossed down by careless humans. The most sophisticated and deceptive nest is that of the Cape penduline tit: a small, nondescript bird. The delicate nest is woven and moulded from grass, feathers and spiders' webs, and whilst building the roof of the dome the bird builds an entrance spout similar to that of the weaver's nest. This is, in fact, a decoy leading nowhere and is

built no doubt to confuse nest-robbing hawks and snakes. The real entrance is tucked under the fake one and on each arrival and departure the tit closes the secret entrance, probably using the spider web to seal it tight. Of all the nest builders, the weavers put the most time and devotion into their intricately woven nests. Each nest consists of several thousand strands torn from long grasses and palm fronds and these are twisted and knotted into subtle shapes that differ with each species. On completion, the nest is actively and noisily advertised by the male, the sole architect, to attract a mate and the small colonies are easily located by their frantic din. Should the male not attract a female, then his work is seen as inadequate and he tears it down and starts again.

Most birds are diurnal, or active by day, but as the sun sets many nocturnal species begin to stir. Since these birds are seldom seen, they have to be identified by their calls. The strident piping calls of the spotted dikkop seem to herald the coming darkness. The six species of nightjar are very hard to spot by day, but their various yelps, churring, trills and twitterings clearly identify each species. Visually the most spectacular is the male pennantwinged nightjar. During the breeding season he grows a pale secondary wing feather over 700 mm long, several times longer than his body. This feather acts as a prominent banner in the evening light to attract a potential mate.

Each of the owls, the nocturnal raptors, has its own distinctive call ranging from the regular five-second-apart chirp of the diminutive scops owl, to the antiphonal duet of a pair of pearlspotted owls and the hoots of the spotted and giant eagle owls. They are still-hunters, their superb night vision and sensitive hearing allowing them to detect the rustles of rodents and insects in the undergrowth so that they can home in on them with unerring accuracy on soft, near-silent wings.

Hwange's birdlife is rich in year-round resident species, but the diversity nearly doubles with the arrival of the migratory birds when the rains start. The phenomenal increase in food brought on by the rains is timed perfectly for the arrival of weary, famished migrants from Eurasia, and a feeding frenzy ensues as they rapidly build up depleted body reserves. Some come to breed, others just to gorge on food. Water collects in temporary pans that attract dozens of species of waterfowl and waders. The waterfowl are mainly localised migrants returning from areas of more reliable surface water in the region to breed in these ideal feeding and nursery areas. The air is filled with the three-syllable whistles of whitefaced duck, and pairs of redbilled and Hottentot teal frantically fly pell-mell to proclaim their territorial boundaries. The large bulbous protrusion on the beak of the male knobbilled duck proclaims his readiness to court and breed. Many of the waders are palearctic wanderers, having bred thousands of kilometres to the north, and species such as ruffs migrate to capitalise on the glut of food. One of the most unusual waders that does breed during the rains is the painted snipe, and this is one of the rare examples in the bird world of role reversal. The female is the more strikingly coloured and she courts various males, leaving her eggs to be incubated and the young to be raised by these drabber males.

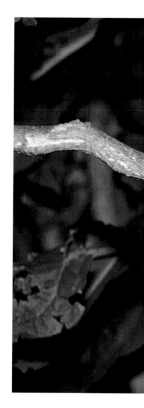

Migratory raptors also have a role to fill during the rainy season and Hwange teems with yellowbilled kites. These opportunistic scavengers cohabit easily with humans and are regular, if somewhat annoying, attractions at the outdoor braai lunch at Hwange Safari Lodge. Masters of aerial manoeuvres, they wheel about the eating area waiting to swoop on any unsuspecting resident's lunch and literally snatch the food from the plates of diners. One particularly impudent kite swooped down onto a visitor's dessert and flew off with red jelly dripping from its talons — not the scrumptious meal it had hoped for!

One of the most spectacular migrant visitors is the brilliant vermilion carmine bee-eater. This bird breeds in large colonies, digging tunnel nests in sandy river banks mainly outside the park for lack of suitable riverine breeding habitat within it. When the adults and fully fledged juveniles hawk insects over the open, grassy areas, along with other incredibly vivid members of the family — the little bee-eater, swallowtailed bee-eater and whitefronted bee-eater — each twig, stump, and termite mound is a mass of colour.

Whilst most tourists come to Hwange to see the spectacular big game, the profusion of birdlife offers a spectacle in its own right. When sitting at a waterhole waiting for animals to come down and drink, or driving around hoping to bump into something special around the next bend, do not be disap-

pointed if things seem quiet. Listen and look — birds are always around. Watching their antics and appreciating their beauty is just as rewarding as watching a herd of elephants at a waterhole. Besides, the appreciation of birds that you develop at Hwange can later be enjoyed in the comfort of your own garden. This is more than can be said for the dwindling game animals. But beware: birdwatching can become obsessive!

Left: *The colourful green pigeon is often found in riverine forest and fruiting fig trees and is hard to detect when feeding high on the forest canopy.* Below: *A bateleur eagle warily approaches the water at Mandavu Dam.* Far left: *The redbilled francolin is common in the Kalahari and its loud, harsh call is a distinctive feature of the bush.*

DIARY OF HWANGE ·

'The dawn had an unseasonable chill, probably thanks to a heavy downpour in the early hours of the morning. Everything was soaked, the sand was soggy and all but the deepest and freshest spoor had been obliterated. Grass and shrubs bent low from the weight of water still dripping copiously from branch and leaf.'

Above: *An oleander hawk moth.*
Main picture: *Unseasonable clouds add contrast to a winter's dusk at Nyamandhlovu Pan.*

JANUARY

Nature's deadly game

I t was a crisp, clear 'champagne' morning as I drove down to Nyamandhlovu Pan, and faint wisps of mist floated up from the bejewelled, sodden earth. Arriving at the pan and ascending the sturdy platform I was able to witness a battle of wills taking place. Three wild dogs from the temporarily resident pack were sprawled on an old termite mound on the opposite side of the pan, playing with what looked like the fresh remains of a small kudu's hind leg. Looking on in interest about 15 m away were two spotted hyenas, obviously eager to partake of these meagre leftovers.

I could not tell whether the kill was the wild dogs' own or if it had been usurped from the hyenas, but the dogs had obviously enjoyed a good meal and the hyenas now felt it was their turn. Hunger overcame their usual reluctance to challenge their adversaries and they pushed too close for the wild dogs to let such impudence go uncontested. One of the dogs sprinted out, nipped a hyena on the rump and chased them for some distance. The dogs were obviously unwilling to be intimidated into handing over their scraps without a show of dominance.

Whilst this skirmish was taking place my attention was grabbed by a far more earnest contest. Two dots zoomed across the sky at high speed from the eastern side of the clearing. Even with the aid of binoculars it

took some time to work out the identity of the protagonists. A Cape turtledove was flying flat out to escape from a male black sparrowhawk in full pursuit.

Rather than jink through the scrub, where the black sparrowhawk has the advantage of manoeuvrability, the Cape turtledove tried to outpace its adversary. It had made the wrong decision. Inexorably the black sparrowhawk musket, as the male is also known, was gaining with each wingbeat. The swift turtledove can outfly most raptors but not a black sparrowhawk. The largest member of the sparrowhawk family in the world, this bird's long-distance speed and stamina makes it the avian equivalent of a heat-seeking missile.

The birds flashed past the platform, each intent on its final goal. The chase wore on but the outcome was surely inevitable. With the black sparrowhawk just centimetres from its final pounce only desperate evasive tactics would save the turtledove now.

Meanwhile the other contest by the pan had just about played itself out. The wild dogs obviously decided that they'd had enough and keeping the hyenas at bay was too much of a chore. As one they trotted off in the direction of their den. The hyenas swiftly moved in and, pulling and tugging, separated skin from bone of the hind leg. They then made off to the security of cover to savour their meagre and hard-won scraps.

Top: *Sunset illuminates a camelthorn near Nyamandhlovu platform in the dusty dry season.* Above: *A Cape turtledove drinks from its own reflection. Flocks of doves attract many predators to the waterhole.* Left: *The water monitor or leguaan, Africa's largest lizard, is a voracious predator in and around the water.*

Right: *A pack of African wild dogs stalk their intended prey prior to the chase.*
Below: *A female golden orb-web spider, one of Africa's largest, spins huge webs between trees and shrubs. Although totally blind, it is a very effective predator.*
Bottom: *An impala ram keeps a watchful eye on his harem.*

FEBRUARY

An endangered predator

The sun hit the horizon and transformed the bush into a dazzling spectacle. A heavy dew made the lush greenery look as if it was hung with gems, lit up by the early morning rays.

As I turned a corner of the gravelled road to Nyamandhlovu, where the dense scrub opens up to a wide expanse of open grassland around the pan, I saw four members of the wild dog pack which had been in the area for some weeks stretched out on a termite mound. Obviously enjoying the warmth of the early sunshine, they looked totally at peace. This tranquil scene soon changed as all four dogs sat up in unison, their large round ears honed in like radars on three more members of the pack emerging from the scrub some 50 m to the east.

As one, the four sunbathers trotted off behind the second group, their gait and demeanour suggesting a keen sense of purpose. Following slowly behind I soon saw a large herd of impala the pack had obviously targeted. Though using the long grass as a screen the dogs did not seem overly concerned with stealth or concealment. One impala saw them and gave a loud piercing alarm call, at which the herd broke and fled in panic.

Now the wild dog pack fanned out and within a pace changed from an extended trot to a full gallop. All but one dog, who remained trotting by the side of my truck. The chase ran the length of the open area and I was able to keep up for most of the way. My companion remained on the blind side of the truck, seemingly uninterested in the exertions of the other members of the pack.

The fleeing impala galloped along in urgent yet graceful intensity. The dogs had not yet singled out a victim but the contest neared its inevitable conclusion. It is uncanny that these efficient hunters can be spread out over a large area and yet act in unison as though through some extrasensory link. An impala was run down by the majority of the pack on the far side of the vlei, but one dog had singled out a young ram and was heading it off in the direction of my truck.

My lethargic companion now showed his true colours. Although he had been running for nearly 3 km he broke cover and sped off, cornering the desperate young impala. Pulling it down, he was soon joined by the second dog and the impala's bleats were rapidly silenced. Three more dogs came to enjoy the plentiful pickings.

The pack retreated to the pan for a rest and a quick drink. Again as one they were up and off in the direction of Main Camp, where the pack had denned down and the dominant pair had a litter of puppies. The dogs settled in the vicinity each year, abandoning their nomadic life for a short while. But as soon as the pups could keep up with the pack, the dogs would resume their usual lifestyle.

MARCH

The vagaries of nature

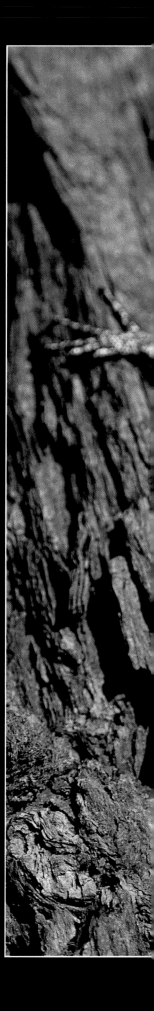

Sitting at the Mandavu picnic site when the bush is parched by drought it is hard to visualise what happened there one hectic night in 1988.

The 1987-88 rainy season had been an average one and the park was lush and green. Prospects of water supplies lasting throughout the dry season seemed reasonable. Early in March the rains usually start to peter out and the slow desiccation begins. This March was not to be normal, though. The heaviest rains of the year fell, and with terrifying force.

The amount of rain varied in different parts of the park, but it was fair to say that the heavens opened up. Sinamatella Rest Camp registered 200 mm in a little over an hour and a half. At about 8.30 that evening a deafening roar signalled that the Sinamatella River was in full flood. And such a flood could only be caused by the breaching of Mandavu Dam.

Next day the extent of the damage could clearly be seen even though it was still raining. The huge earth wall retaining the dam had completely disappeared! The force of the water escaping the dam was mind-boggling. Tall trees had simply been swept away, and a large swathe of flattened bush marked the line of inundation. The dam, which covered several square kilometres, had simply disappeared, leaving a sea of mud behind. Birds were congregating to take advantage of others' misfortune

— nature does not let a windfall go begging. Exposed mudflats yielded a bonanza of insects, larvae, molluscs, crustaceans, amphibians, reptiles and fish. And the birds weren't the only ones taking advantage. Below the spot where the dam wall used to be, a large pool of water was seething with barbel. Spoor around the pool showed that a leopard was making the most of an easy opportunity.

Mandavu Dam is the largest open water in Hwange and it is especially important as a source of water to the dry mopane-covered hills around Sinamatella. The water being lost as the river flowed through the breached wall could scarcely be afforded.

Within two days a bulldozer had been loaned by the Wankie Colliery Company Limited, one of the many acts of assistance rendered to the park over the years by the coal miners. Soon the wall was plugged and then rebuilt. Enough water was still flowing into the repaired dam to ensure that it would not dry up before the end of the coming dry season.

With the dam wall complete a unique aquatic environment was saved from devastation. The crocodiles and hippos were saved, and fish trapped in pools below the wall were caught and returned to the main dam. The main face of the wall was covered with rock to prevent crocodiles digging lairs in the soft earth, a habit that has been blamed for several small dam wall failures in the past.

Top: *Runoff water starts to accumulate behind the hastily repaired breach of Mandavu Dam.* Above: *A broiling mass of sharptoothed catfish or barbel in the drying pan are at risk to predators. Some may survive in the deep, moist mud until the rains come.* Left: *A male blueheaded tree agama.*

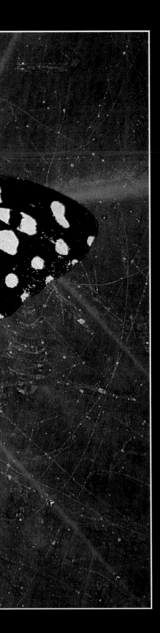

APRIL

The change of seasons

Autumn in the African bush is not a clearly defined season as in the northern hemisphere. In Africa the transition is, as in all things, dictated by the rains. By April the rains are normally over and the annual cycle of life has turned full circle.

Hwange does not have a spectacular autumn, but the leaves of many trees do change colour and drop. First to fall are the baobab, mukwa and syringa, all turning a soothing golden yellow, whilst the spectacular kuduberry stands out in bright crimson.

This time of year also marks the end of the time of plenty for browser and grazer and now the lessons of survival become essential. The first chill is felt in the morning air and on certain days spectacular morning mists blanket the pans and vleis. On mornings such as these an eerie silence pervades the veld, occasionally punctuated by the howl of a lone jackal, as the rising sun confers a golden-red aura on the earth.

One such golden morning will remain etched on my memory forever. I was parked near Dom Pan when Stompie, a large female white rhino, and her young calf nearly walked into my Land Rover. The dense mists and eerie silence seemed to have disoriented the rhinos as their superb sense of smell should have warned them of my presence. Unperturbed, Stompie grazed close by for some minutes then lay down to allow the calf to suckle. Stompie was so named because of her damaged anterior (front) horn which was stunted and very slow growing and an easy means of identification. She was quite at ease with vehicles and was regularly seen near Main Camp.

The white rhino was hunted to extinction in Zimbabwe in the early 1890s but reintroduced from Natal in the 1960s. The extensive calcrete grassland areas sweeping from Ngamo through Malalolo and Linkwasha to the Kennedy Vlei and Main Camp, then on to Nyamandhlovu, past Guvalala and on to Shumba Pans, were the ideal habitat for the white rhino and they bred up well. The population grew to about 200 animals and their future looked healthy, if only for a while.

It is poignant to reflect back to that golden morning when Stompie and her calf grazed peacefully just feet away from me. I later saw Stompie stealing a quick drink in the dead of night, a creature now living in perpetual fear in her own domain.

The following month the carcasses of Stompie and her calf were found in thick scrub not far north of Dom Pan. They had died in a hail of poachers' bullets.

These are the last days of the rhino. What will satisfy the greed of those who control this abomination? Will it be the ivory of Hwange's elephants? And can we protect them any better than the poor old rhino?

Above: *The citrus swallowtail butterfly is one of dozens of species of gorgeous eye-catching moths and butterflies found in Hwange.*
Left: *White rhino in the misty early morning.* Far left: *The leopard tortoise is the most common tortoise found in Hwange.*

MAY

Is there no retreat?

The lead Land Rover ground to a halt and the tracker, Shorty, jumped out to check the huge mound of fresh elephant dung. The spoor clearly indicated that three elephant bulls had passed this way only a couple of hours earlier. This random act of passage had sealed the fate of one of the elephants, as we were on a training cull. Ron Thomson, then warden of Hwange, led the small column now following the spoor through the thick scrub. The aim was to teach two young and relatively inexperienced officers all the aspects of management, including culling.

Within 15 minutes we had tracked the trio down and were so close behind them that the cloyingly pungent smell of fresh elephant dung was like a physical presence. The bulls were moving through a particularly dense stand of scrub and we could hear them but not yet see them. Apart from the odd snap of a branch, most of the noise produced was not from eating but digesting. Elephants produce spectacular tummy rumbles, surpassed in loudness only by their flatulence!

Ron and I moved in closer, followed by Ivan Ncube as there was no longer any need for Shorty's skills. Twenty metres ahead a huge backside receded through a parting wall of scrub. As the bulls moved we moved, covering our noise with the racket they made. A few metres more and the bush opened up, the wind changed direction and the bulls had our scent. At this point I realised that there was not a single substantial tree, bush or termite mound in the vicinity to provide cover if the bulls panicked and charged. The two bulls in front made off into the thick cover just in front of them but the rear bull moved off to his left. On seeing us he adopted the threat posture known as 'standing tall' and thereby offered Ron the chance for a frontal brain shot. The split second Ron fired the bull shook his head in warning that he intended to charge.

The 510 grain bullet of a Winchester .458 Magnum has an enormous impact velocity, and though the bullet missed the brain by a fraction it was sufficient to knock the bull on his haunches. Groggily the bull regained his feet and Ron reloaded. Before the bull could start a final charge the second bullet found its mark. It was all over. A brain shot kills instantly and the bull's huge legs had collapsed, leaving him sprawled out on the earth. Cautiously approaching the lifeless form, Ron tested for eye reflex and ascertained that a third bullet was not required.

Looking at this lone, forlorn carcass I could not help but wonder where it will all end. Has our planet any space left for this noble animal and do we really care enough to save them anyway? Even in Hwange, is there no refuge for the elephant?

Above right: *The end, but hopefully not of the species.*
Right: *A mature bull is slain by a brain shot, which is instantaneous.*
Far right: *The beautiful emerald-coloured fruit chafer beetle is one of many spectacular insects found in Hwange.*

Top: *A tour guide feeds a presidential elephant with acacia pods — a unique experience but under no circumstances to be emulated by the public.* Right: *The dominant bull always takes the 'pole' position for the clean water direct from the borehole.* Above: *The conspicuous markings of the male dot-underwing moth — a nocturnal moth common in Hwange.*

JUNE

The presidential herd

S itting in an open Land Rover feet away from a wild elephant may seem a fit pursuit for the deranged, but only with such intimate contact does one really appreciate the magnificence of the world's largest land mammal.

This rare privilege can be enjoyed by visitors to Hwange Safari Lodge or one of its exclusive camps at Sikumi, Sable Valley or Konondo Bush Camp. The Safari Lodge is situated on private land and land leased from the Zimbabwe Forestry Commission that adjoins Hwange National Park and forms a buffer between the park and private farmland and communal areas.

Thanks to the dedication and perseverance of Alan Elliot and his many guides over the past 20 years, a nucleus of 17 harassed and persecuted crop-raiding elephants has been built up to a stable population. The present complement of about 300 elephants centres on the flexible breed herd. The males, being wanderers at heart, come and go as nature dictates.

Through rigid protection from poaching, snaring and undue harassment from over-eager guides, Elliot and his team have habituated these animals to accept the close presence of vehicles and their occupants. Years of patience has paid off as the elephants now calmly approach vehicles, continuing their normal activities without agitation or threat. Because of this special and unique relationship

between man and beast Elliot successfully petitioned Zimbabwe's president, Robert Mugabe, to issue a special decree to protect the herd from outside interference and hopefully ensure their long-term stability. The presidential herd, as they are now known, offer scientists a unique opportunity to study elephants up close.

Even the cows, normally very protective of their offspring, will allow a newborn calf to closely approach and inspect a vehicle without any of the usual threat displays and trumpeting which mean imminent danger.

Sitting at one of the estate's waterholes and watching the presidential herd take its daily dip can provide hours of enjoyment. In the dry season the herd strides purposefully to the waterhole and passes vehicles totally unconcerned, intent only on the cool, refreshing water. The bulls accompanying the herd usually head straight for the outlet of the borehole with its fresh, clear water. The cows and calves generally avoid this hotly contested 'pole' position at the outlet and go to the waterhole proper. Bathing and frolicking at the waterhole, the elephants present a picture of total contentment. The rigid hierarchy seems to be relaxed and young and old alike enjoy a playful dip.

The presidential herd is a unique group of elephants that could provide scientists and conservationists with the insights to help save this beleaguered giant from extinction.

JULY

Murphy's law of photography

Winter was in full swing and the effects of the dry season becoming more noticeable. The colours of autumn had been replaced by the stark hues of winter. Bleached tawny yellow grass contrasted with the brown leaves of trees that had not yet shed their leaves and the stark grey trunks of those that had. I was at the platform at Big Toms Pan, an almost ideal spot for photography in winter.

The more open grassy areas near Robins Camp, close to the Botswana border, are favoured by the endangered roan antelope and several small family groups came down to drink, casting near-perfect reflections on the still surface of the pan. The roan were joined by sable, zebra, kudu and impala while a family of warthog enjoyed a squelchy mud bath as well as a drink. Big Toms also attracts a retinue of reedbuck, common in this area of the park. Solitary males and small groups of dominant males with their females and young filed down well-established game trails to drink. We were not the only ones paying attention to the reedbuck, though. About half a kilometre to the west a pair of adult male cheetah slunk up to a large anthill and, standing atop this prominent vantage point, watched with obvious intent.

The cheetah may well have hunted here regularly and observed the reedbucks' regular movements so they could use this knowledge to their advantage. Slowly they moved off, all but disappearing in the long golden grass. Skirting a herd of elephant in the streambed, they must have crossed the Big Toms undetected for we soon got the occasional glimpse of the pair stealthily using the cover of the large stand of mopane trees. The cheetah were now less than 100 m from the unsuspecting reedbuck. I could hardly contain a growing excitement: at long last I would be lucky enough to watch the entire sequence of the cheetah's legendary hunting skills.

With an appalling sense of timing a troop of baboons emerged from the mopane stand and one of the leading sentry males wandered between the cheetah and their prey. The resulting barks, shrieks and screams of the panic-stricken troop would have woken the dead as they crashed back into the mopane trees. The commotion was immediately picked up by the reedbuck who were in full flight in a flash.

The cheetah knew that the game was up and flopped down in the shade for a short rest before returning to the distant antheap to doze in the sun, probably knowing that the reedbuck or something else would be back soon enough.

Unfortunately I was not there to witness it, though. All I could do was reflect on Murphy's law of photography: 'If something can possibly go wrong, be assured it will.'

Left: *The magnificent golden-maned male lion took no part in the boisterous game.* Below: *Who's watching whom? A young chacma baboon seems intrigued by all the attention he's getting.* Bottom: *The startling eye patterns of the dot-underwing caterpillar are the opposite of camouflage and advertise its unpleasant taste to would-be predators.*

AUGUST

Living dangerously

The night had been relatively quiet at our camp at the picnic site at Ngweshla Pan. Several arguments between bull elephants at the pan had rent the still night air. The roars of distant lion and a few whoops from prowling hyenas all added to the flavour of a night spent under the star-studded canopy of the African sky.

In the early hours a white rhino bull woke me and my son Douglas by rubbing his horn vigorously on the corner post of the fence, setting the wire strands twanging. Douglas, at nine years of age, was a veteran of camping out in the wilderness areas and was not unduly fazed by such an occurrence. As the first traces of red lit up the eastern horizon the lions started roaring again, obviously much closer this time. It is amazing how far a lion's roar travels, especially in a cold, still dawn. A certain trepidation seeps into the subconscious mind, no doubt a throwback to primeval times when our ancestors lived in perpetual fear of the supreme predator.

Our lions were some distance away and were vocal for a long time. As we were about to leave, the roaring of the lions was joined by the screams of numerous chacma baboon, obviously in a great deal of distress. We had to find out why.

We soon found out the cause of the commotion. A pride of 14 lions was slowly heading away from the pan to thicker cover to lay up for the day.

The cause of the ruckus was the cubs, who were playing a very innovative game of tag with a troop of baboons. The troop of 20 or so baboons were firmly ensconced in a large African ebony tree growing out of a huge old termite mound. The cubs gathered around the termite mound and the baboons hurled abuse at them.

Whenever the cubs got bored with this and moved off to follow the adults, a couple of more adventurous baboons would drop out of the tree and sit on the termite mound. The cubs would sprint back to the mound, sending the baboons scampering back into the tree and triggering off a new bout of frenzied screaming.

This amusing 'king-of-the-castle' act was repeated nine times, much to the disgust of the male lion, who would repeatedly call his family itinerants to no avail. On one sortie a larger cub managed a leap of herculean proportions and succeeded in swatting the tail of one of the baboons perched in the lower branches. No longer feeling as safe as before, the baboon shot to the top of the tree and sat out the proceedings.

The game continued until the rising sun warmed things up sufficiently for the cubs to realise it was becoming hard work. The pride at last re-formed and went to seek shade for a day of rest, while the troop of baboons fanned out to start its daily foraging routine.

SEPTEMBER

Aquatic hyenas

T he dry season was progressing and though the chill of early mornings was still wintry the days were getting steadily hotter, starting the build-up to the rains some two months hence. Most of the seasonal pans had by now dried up and the animals depended solely on the artificial water supplies from boreholes pumped to certain pans.

I was going to spend the day at one such artificially supplied pan called Guvalala, which is noted for big elephant bulls. I was prepared to sit for the day and hope for the best, little aware of the unusual behaviour I was to witness.

A large clan of hyenas, resident in the vicinity of Guvalala, have proved to be highly efficient predators and not the skulking, cowardly scavengers they are often thought to be. This clan regularly cooperates to hunt and bring down large antelope. On this morning five of the clan were lying at the water's edge. I initially thought they were just cooling off after an arduous hunt or cleaning themselves after a gory meal. Unconcerned at my arrival, they lounged around in the shallow water for some time. One eventually rose and, instead of trotting off to the den to sleep away the heat of the day, proceeded to wade belly-deep into the pan. Hyenas occasionally cache food in shallow water away from the attention of lions and vultures, and as Guvalala was free of crocodiles it would make

an ideal aquatic larder. But to my surprise, the hyena dived under the surface and remained submerged for over five seconds.

This behaviour, more fitting for an otter or a hippopotamus, was repeated by two more of the clan. After each dive the hyenas would surface with a morsel which they would swallow, then continue their diving. The water was deep enough to require considerable effort in remaining submerged for any length of time. Occasionally a hyena would tear off more than it could swallow and would have to swim ashore to gobble down its prize, if those not diving at the time did not steal it.

The original group was joined by two more of the clan and all seven joined in the diving activities, though not at the same time. Every now and again the hoof of whatever was being eaten would clear the surface but never long enough to reveal what animal it belonged to. Eventually four of them joined forces to pull the prey out, and the horns of a magnificent kudu bull broke the surface. But try as they might the four could not drag the carcass out.

Who could tell what dramas had unfolded to create the unusual scenes that I was lucky enough to witness. Many antelope retreat to the relative safety of the water when pursued by predators, but how such a huge, strong animal became entangled and submerged we will never know.

Top: *A magnificent kudu bull poses at Guvalala Pan.*
Above: *Two of the 'aquatic' hyenas diving for a meal.*
Right: *The bateleur eagle, acrobat of the African skies.*

Top: *The strikingly handsome martial eagle, the largest of Africa's eagles.*
Right: *The herald or redlipped snake is back-fanged, and though the venom is mild, it is enough to immobilise prey.*
Below: *The red velvet mite is a subterranean arachnid that emerges in large numbers with the first rains.*

OCTOBER

Master of the skies

I n Hwange in mid-October the heat is an inescapable, physical presence, strong enough to drain the last reserves of energy and life-giving moisture from all but the strongest. Temperatures regularly soar over 40 °C. Cumulus clouds form each afternoon, only hinting at rains soon to come, at times even grudgingly releasing a small shower. Few of these ever reach the ground to provide respite from the oppressive heat. Small wonder that locals refer to October as 'suicide month'. On days such as this life nearly grinds to a halt. Even at the pans and waterholes, life seems to have given up.

One such day at Salt Pans several impala rams were clinging listlessly to the scant patch of shade provided by a straggly stand of tree wisteria.

For several hours the only movement was from a few birds feeding at the pan's edge. Fitful gusts of wind blew irritating clouds of dust, and the occasional dust devil brought the impalas nervously out of their collective torpor.

Just when the heat had nearly sapped my patience, a bustling phalanx of motion burst forth from the mopane scrub ringing the shrunken pan. A covey of 57 helmeted guineafowl waddled down to the water's edge across the 300 m of open ground in a long single file. Once there, it took several minutes for these energetic characters — evenly

fanned around a small inlet — to slake their thirst.

As soon as the entire flock had its fill, the orderly procession started the return journey to the relative safety of the surrounding mopane scrub. Several birds broke from the column and, sensing some danger, issued their staccato warning call. The previously orderly file of guineafowl instantly turned into a rout of blind panic. The guineafowl took to the air and sought the closest possible cover, but not quickly enough. With wind reverberating through primary wingtips and alula, a magnificent martial eagle swooped down on the melee below, deftly braking, tossing up and plucking a tail-ender out of the throng in one fluid movement. The last frantic flutters of the doomed bird were quickly terminated by the fearsome grip of foot and talon.

The martial eagle effortlessly glided to earth while the remaining guineafowl found cover. Much calling ensued as the group re-formed.

As the hapless victim spent out its last few spasms, the huge eagle lazily started to pluck away its breast feathers, readying a nice, plump meal. This encounter, which plays itself out many times a day at Hwange, epitomises the realities of survival in the bush. As the guineafowl's feathers blew away in the wind and its blood soaked into the Kalahari sands, the martial eagle had ensured her food requirements for the next day or so.

NOVEMBER

And the rains came

The slow build-up to the rains seemed unending. The intensity of the heat grew daily and the searing sun felt like burning needles on the skin. Night brought little relief as the massive cumulus thunderclouds rumbled across the sky creating fearsome electrical storms. Lightning struck the ground as if seeking refuge from the congestion aloft, each bolt capable of starting a horrific conflagration in the tinder-dry bush.

The toll of the long, hard dry season was all too evident. The area around nearby Somavhundla Pan was now totally devoid of vegetation as far back as the distant treeline. The comings and goings of the animals had churned up the loose, dry sand. The seasonal pans were dusty expanses of caked mud, baked iron hard.

Animals congregated round the artificial waterholes as the small diesel pumps valiantly pumped cool, life-giving water from deep underground. They supplied water 24 hours a day, but still demand often exceeded supply. The previous night over 500 elephants had visited the concrete trough next to the pan and within two hours it was drained dry. The air was rent by distant rolls of thunder and shrill shrieks and trumpeting as dozens of elephants fought for a desperately needed drink.

Harry, the lone resident male hippo, spent his days wallowing in the gooiest part of the pan, a certain death trap to many animals, but not enough to worry Harry, whose bulk and strength allowed him to dredge channels wherever he pleased.

The next day we found a young roan antelope trapped in the thick ooze of a nearby pan, caught by his desperate need for water. With the help of extra hands and a stout rope, we managed to free the animal.

Strained to the limit, the clouds could no longer hold back. First came a howling wind and then a hushed silence, punctuated by the occasional splat of a heavy drop of rain raising a puff of dust. Crashes of thunder seemed to explode just feet away and the darkness was pierced by electric blue spears of lightning.

As the drops of rain increased in crescendo, everyone willed the heavens to open. Despite the intensity of an African storm, the smell of that first rain is etched into the psyche of all who live in Africa. It signals the end of hard times and is the harbinger of a new season of growth, birth and reproduction.

The rainfall was by now a constant, distant drumming. Torrents poured from roofs and eaves, clearing away months of accumulated dust. Another sudden blast of wind came and then the storm hit with a vengeance as if making up for eight months of inactivity. In one frantic, turbulent night, the rains had finally arrived and the bush's cycle of life set in motion once again.

Top: *The roan calf trapped in the cloying mud of a drying up pan.* Above: *The heavens open and the waterholes get a new lease of life.* Right: *Elephants drink clean water from a borehole outlet.*

Far right: The giant land snail, one of Africa's largest gastropods, is common during the rainy season.
Right: When the first rains fall the grey tree frog, an arboreal species, creates white foamy egg-nests in branches overhanging pans. When ready, the tadpoles break free and land in the water below.
Below: The waterhole is the very centre of Hwange's existence and essential to the variety of life found in the bush.

DECEMBER

The pan

Good rains had been falling for weeks and the transformation at Hwange was remarkable. At Dwarf Goose Pan — a fair-sized seasonal pan next to the main road between Main Camp and Sinamatella — the contrast was startling. Where dust devils had swirled only weeks before, now dabchicks dived and blackwinged stilts strode about in a constant search for food.

To many, a pan is nothing more than a depression that fills with water where animals come down to slake their thirst. How wrong a cursory glance can be. As runoff from the rains accumulates in the pan, the nutrients left behind in the mud in the form of vegetation detritus, dung and urine, are all released into the water. The pan becomes a broth of organic food which, warmed by the sun, triggers a spectacular explosion of life. Algae, phytoplankton and zooplankton at the base of the food chain support progressively more advanced life forms.

A remarkable inhabitant is the fairy shrimp, which miraculously appears in swarms within days of the first puddle forming. These crustaceans proliferate into millions in suitable conditions, surviving until the pools dry out again. The parents die, but not before preparing the next generation. Millions of eggs lie in the dust, encapsulated for protection, and remain dormant for up to 20 years if conditions demand.

Dormant vegetation also takes on a new lease of life with remarkable rapidity. Water lilies, sedges and sawgrass all suddenly appear in their respective niches. Amphibians also seem to sprout with the first rains and a remarkable array of toads, reed frogs, bullfrogs, painted frogs, rain frogs and tree frogs emerges from the moist and softened earth.

A peculiar feature of many pans is a white froth hanging from overhanging branches and shrubs. This is the spawn mass of the grey tree frogs which call, mate and spawn in the trees. The rich variety of food in the pan attracts many reptilian predators. The swarms of tadpoles draw small snakes such as the herald snake, while cobras are attracted to adult frogs and toads. The African rock python is drawn like a magnet to such pans and its size and crushing power allow it to extend its prey base to waterfowl and small mammals.

Whereas most inhabitants of the pan remain hidden to the casual observer, the birdlife cannot go unnoticed. Dozens of species of migrants head for Hwange — some after mind-boggling journeys.

The pan is essential to the well-being of Hwange and its inhabitants, but its facets are many, varied and at times not very obvious. It is, albeit temporarily, home to a complex array of interdependent creatures and far more than just a drinking place for the spectacular big game.

CHAPTER 9

CONSERVATION

*'Man always kills the things he loves, and so we the
pioneers have killed our wilderness. Some say we had to.
Be that as it may, I am glad I shall never be young without wild
country to be young in. Of what avail are forty freedoms
without a blank spot on the map?'*

Aldo Leopold

THE MANAGEMENT
OF HWANGE'S ECOSYSTEMS

The topic of the management of Hwange is currently, to all intents and purposes, theoretical. The programme of practical management carried out until the late 1970s gradually ground to a halt as financial strangulation was applied by an unsympathetic central treasury. Management comprises many facets including water supply, fire management, road maintenance, firebreak maintenance, tourism development, soil conservation, anti-poaching activities and the various aspects of wildlife management.

Left: *There is never enough water in Hwange, and storm clouds do not always fulfil their promise of rain.* Above: *Adventurous tourists can really get the feel of the bush on backpacking trails of one to four nights through the park.*

Water

The provision of boreholes is the most important management function for the wellbeing of Hwange's wildlife. The park's erratic rainfall pattern means there is not enough surface water to last throughout the dry season. In addition, the sporadic distribution of rainfall can leave areas of the park bone-dry early on in the season, thereby increasing competition for food and water at the remaining water points, with resultant extra pressure on the vegetation in the vicinity.

The first boreholes were drilled as far back as 1939 and gradually a total of 42 boreholes augmented the seasonal supply to most of Hwange's vast area. There are over 120 medium to large pans that hold a reasonable amount of water in most seasons, but the provision of borehole water aims to avoid heavy concentrations with the resultant degradation in these areas.

In addition to boreholes, the water supply programme also included the damming of several watercourses, mainly in the northern watershed, for additional reliable, all-season water points. In all, 13 earth wall dams were built along some of the better defined watercourses. Half a dozen windmills also remain in the park, often out of commission for lack of parts and maintenance. Wind power provides cheap, regular water supplies all year round, but these pumps produce small volumes and can only be regarded as a means of augmenting supply.

The groundwater tapped by these boreholes is essential to Hwange's wildlife and was originally thought to be a vast, unending resource constantly supplied by the inland delta of the Okavango River. In fact, the source of supply to the intricate system of underground streams and rivers is far more complex than this. The quality of the water is also highly variable. Dissolved mineral salts, mainly sodium and lime, make the water at some boreholes so salty that it is unpalatable to humans, whereas other boreholes have nearly pure water. Fortunately, the saltier the water the greater its attraction to wildlife!

Long-term extraction from these underground water reserves seems to disprove the theory that the water table is supplied from such a reliable source as the Okavango. The depth of boreholes can vary considerably from as little as 20 m below the surface to well over 150 m deep. Some boreholes are now running dry and have to be deepened to ensure water supplies continue. Little research has been carried out by hydrologists on the percentage of Hwange's underground water resources, but over the border, in Botswana, far more research has been undertaken to try to solve the mysteries of this treasure locked beneath the Kalahari sands.

Scientists can find out how often the groundwater is replenished by determining the level of tritium, a radioactive isotope of hydrogen. The advent of nuclear technology helped give a reliable indication of age of water, as the atmospheric level of tritium

Right: Stately bulls lose all sense of dignity as they frolic in a full Kanondo Pan. Below: The poor state of repair of the pumphouse at Ngweshla bears testimony to the chronic lack of government funds for basic maintenance at Hwange.

soared on account of thermonuclear testing, which peaked in 1963. Tritium testing of the water in Botswana showed that 40 per cent of boreholes were being replenished. Carbon 14 dating also showed, however, that some boreholes tapped water which had not been replenished for over 30 000 years.

Replenishment through downward percolation of rainwater is also unreliable as 1,5 cm of rainfall soaks the sand to a depth of 20 cm, a ratio known as the 'field capacity'. Hwange's average rainfall would not allow a field capacity penetration beyond a depth of 6 m. Dr John Vogel of the Council for Scientific and Industrial Research in Pretoria suggests that this field capacity could be further enhanced by successive layers of rainfall. If sufficient rain fell in a good season, the deeper levels of soaked-in rain would lie beyond the sun's desiccating effect and moisture could not be brought back to the surface by capillarity.

No doubt some of Hwange's borehole water is of ancient origin and is in effect being abused. This water should be viewed as a limited resource. Other boreholes seem to be regularly recharged from a reliable source by lateral recharge, obviously linked to faulting systems in the bedrock buried far beneath the carpet of Kalahari sands.

Unfortunately the degree of variation of the boreholes remains largely unknown so the water supply cannot be predicted. Without the boreholes, Hwange could not exist as we know it and the park would only be able to support a small fraction of its current complement of animals. An alternative solution, known as the Hwange National Park Management Plan, proposes relocating boreholes to new sites at other seasonal pans. Not only will this relieve feeding pressure in sensitive areas and guarantee water supplies for the wildlife, but it will also buy time until the day funds permit a full investigation of the mysteries of Hwange's subterranean hydraulics.

Soil

Soil conservation was an important aspect of the park's management in the 1970s and early 1980s, particularly in the Sinamatella region. This area was originally a ranch and was incorporated into the park decades ago. The management of the veld during the ranching days was particularly bad and extensive sheet and gulley erosion wreaked havoc, especially on open, grassy vleis. This period of devastation is all too evident today and many mopane trees stand free on exposed roots. Headwater erosion has carved a steep gulley the full length of the vlei.

To counter this, rock and bush bolsters follow contours in order to collect runoff silt and plant debris, providing shade to the soil crust to allow moisture to remain long enough to encourage seed germination. The problem in the Sinamatella region is, however, getting worse. The degraded areas are currently doubling in size every six years and now cover nearly 200 km². Owing to the funding crisis, all soil conservation exercises have halted except for the protection of roads from washaways and gulley erosion. A vicious cycle is in operation with poor plant cover causing trees to die as the impoverished soil's capacity to

cured or at least held in check, but it is certain that the rate of degradation would have been quicker if the area had been left to domestic livestock utilisation.

Fire control

Another aspect of Hwange's management that has fallen by the wayside is fire management and firebreak maintenance. Attitudes to fire have changed drastically over the years and fire is now considered a useful tool in wildlife management if used judiciously. Fire management utilises 'cool burns' early in the season to improve veld quality by removing moribund grass and shrub growth, so promoting regeneration and releasing nutrients back into the cycle at a faster rate. In fact, some species of plants actually rely on fire as an essential part of their life cycle.

The term 'cool burn' is no misnomer and

Below left: *Fire, if judiciously used, is a useful tool in veld management, but when the bush is tinder-dry before the rains it can cause tremendous damage in open woodlands.*
Below: *Large impala herds in the Sinamatella region have contributed to the particularly bad soil erosion in the area.*
Below right: *Elephants have the right of way in Hwange.*

absorb and retain moisture diminishes. Existing water attracts many animals, and the large numbers of impala are particularly detrimental to the soil. Not only do they exert a heavy feeding pressure on grasses, shrubs and young trees, but in areas of regular concentrations such as watering points, their sharp hooves act like miniature hoes, breaking the soil surface and thus increasing the loss of soil moisture and damaging and destroying delicate root structures, particularly of annual grasses.

The Sinamatella erosion problem was not created by wildlife, but by human error. The cessation of soil management means no one can say for sure if the problem was being

means burning early in the dry season when vegetation is sufficiently moist to prevent damage to growing tissue, so that the fire just removes dead and decaying material. Such burns also have the beneficial effect of eradicating pests and parasites such as ticks and mange mites.

Fire control aims to prevent 'hot burns', which usually occur late in the dry season when major conflagrations can be easily sparked off. They can cause tremendous damage in tinder-dry woodlands. Such hot burns are extremely difficult and dangerous to contain and it is vital to maintain firebreaks to allow back-burning to control such wild fires.

A well-established hot burn is a fearsome sight, generating convectional winds which help sustain the fire; sparks and firebrands carried by these gale-force winds help the fire to advance in leaps and bounds. This helps to create the patchwork quilt of burnt areas, a mosaic created by the path of the maelstrom.

One area of the park, between Boss Long One and Guvalala, was once set aside for regular small controlled hot burns from 1969 until the early 1980s. This area, a few square kilometres in extent, was bordered by the main tar road and passers-by were invited to compare the vegetation of the protected bush with that of the bush regularly affected by hot burns. A quick look to the left and the right showed a stark contrast, but although the road sign remains, a decade of regeneration has left very little difference on casual observation. The regenerative power of the bush is perhaps more remarkable than we think.

Tourism

Management of tourists and their facilities is a continuous task for parks personnel. The maintenance of accommodation and facilities such as picnic sites is essential to ensure that the tourist receives value for money. With the current price structure, Zimbabwe's national parks must give the best value anywhere in the world. The various camp wardens and staff are to be commended for their dedication and commitment in the upkeep of the camps over the past financially strapped decade.

Since its inception, Hwange has developed tourism on a peripheral basis; the further one goes into the park, the less human influence is noticeable. In fact the major portion of the park is designated as a wilderness area where tourism development is restricted to the barest minimum and casual visitors are not allowed to enter. Again lack of funds prevents any fur-

Wildlife management

ther development, if any were planned. Hwange's road system is inadequate at this time to support further development and many gravel roads are in a poor state of repair. A visitor in a family saloon would be well advised to confirm with the tourist office in each of the camps which are the best roads to use.

Wildlife management

The management of the park's wildlife is yet another victim of inadequate funding. This involves many disciplines such as chemical and mechanical capture of certain species to restock other areas where they have been depleted in their natural habitat. Hwange has been both beneficiary — in the case of rhinos — and benefactor, as in the case of sable and roan antelopes. Such exercises are costly in

terms of expense and manpower, whether it be a darting programme or capture by corralling in a boma.

One of the more recent capture operations held in Hwange was the removal of some crocodiles in the mid-1980s. Crocodiles introduced to the pans on the Kalahari sands in the early days of the park bred readily and

Above: *Hwange has a healthy population of sable antelope and the park has acted as benefactor in a number of restocking programmes.*
Left: *Big Five trophy hunting, organised for paying clients, is an important money earner for conservation efforts.*

were creating an unnatural predation level at permanent pans. The crocodile were captured for release to crocodile breeding farms, part of a healthy industry in Zimbabwe supplying the international demand for crocodile leather. A by-product of this utilisation is a unique Zimbabwean hors d'oeuvre, crocodile tails.

The genetic pool provided by a well-run national park can be an essential source of species in demand for restocking other depleted national parks and game-ranching concerns. Commercial hunting, whether it is hunting for trophies by high fee paying clients or for saleable by-products, such as venison and exotic hides, is an important foreign currency earner for Zimbabwe. All in all, hunting brings in a great deal of money for the government, commercial companies and, more encouragingly, for the local people through Operation Campfire.

PROTECTING THE ELEPHANTS
Africa's poaching holocaust

'If there is any doubt about a decision concerning the fate of wildlife, let the benefit of the doubt always be in favour of the wildlife ...'

(Prince Bernhard of the Netherlands at the opening ceremony of the landmark CITES Conference, Lausanne, Switzerland, October 1989.)

The parks staff at Hwange have tried their best to combat poaching over the years, but the hopelessly inadequate financial vote given by the government to the Department of National Parks and Wildlife Services has hamstrung their efforts. Although a lot of money has been raised both locally and internationally and given to the parks in the form of much-needed equipment ranging from heli-copters to sleeping bags and water bottles, the hard cash for vehicle running costs and salaries was not there when it was most needed.

Most of the hardware essential for extensive para-military operations was earmarked for the lower Zambezi Valley for the much publicised 'Operation Stronghold', to protect the areas populated by the black rhino (at the time the largest population of black rhino in Africa). This operation attempted to combat poaching by engaging the poachers in military action, but even the 'shoot to kill' policy followed by the anti-poaching patrols did not stop rhino losses. In the mid-1980s an extensive relocation programme, involving the chemical capture, or darting, of hundreds of rhino, was implemented. The rhino were

Right: *Part of the presidential herd dust down in the fine alkaline soil of the Dete Vlei.*

moved to national parks and private sanctuaries, difficult for Zambian poachers to invade.

This policy did not succeed in keeping the poachers out, however, and today both the Zambezi Valley and Hwange are virtually devoid of rhino, whether black or white, in any significant numbers. The few isolated survivors remain as a testament to a major failure for conservation in southern Africa, and the Zimbabwean government must accept its share of the blame in this debacle. Not only have we lost a truly magnificent species, but we have cheated future generations out of the significant tourist revenues such animals generate.

There have been no recorded incidents of elephant or rhino poaching in Hwange for several years but ivory poaching is still occurring in the the lower Zambezi Valley. Though prices are deflated there is still a demand for ivory, and stockpiles of poached ivory grow in anticipation of the trading ban being lifted. In any event, illegal ivory still worms its way into the international market.

There can no longer be any doubt that the cessation of trade in ivory voted for by the delegates to the Lausanne Conference in 1989 saved Africa's elephants from annihilation. The resolution was passed by a majority of 76 votes, 11 against (including Zimbabwe) and four abstentions. This resolution was maintained at the 1994 CITES meeting in Fort Lauderdale, USA. The resultant tenfold drop in the value of ivory from US$30,00 to US$3,00 a kilogram meant that the poachers no longer had a massive incentive to kill elephants and the death rates dropped to almost zero within a year. For instance, in Tsavo National Park, Kenya, three elephants a day were poached for their ivory in 1989, the year of the ban, whereas no elephants were lost to poachers in the whole of 1991.

Today the international public views the marketing of ivory and elephant by-products as morally repugnant. Unfortunately this is not the case in Zimbabwe which, along with South Africa and Botswana, is vigorously trying to re-establish an international trade in ivory. These countries have stockpiles of ivory obtained from culling operations and argue that they should be allowed to trade in it because it was not obtained from poaching.

When ivory trading was still legal, however, the punitive monitoring efforts of organisa-

Above: *Sign of the times — a large bull with a bullet wound from a small-calibre rifle. Though the wound does not seem to bother him, the thick hide often heals over sores leaving them to fester internally.* Right: *Large bull elephants are particularly vulnerable to the poacher's gun and in some areas the loss of these members of the herd has resulted in a drop in breeding.*

tions such as CITES and TRAFFIC failed miserably to control the trade, stem the loss of elephants to poaching across Africa, or even nail down individuals or governments exploiting the numerous loopholes. The situation was so lamentable that Burundi, which did not possess a single living elephant, was one of Africa's principal exporters of ivory. South Africa was also exporting ivory far in excess of tonnages it could legitimately account for by culling in the Kruger National Park.

It was not only governments, or more often high-ranking officials abusing their positions, who sanctioned and profited from this illegal trade. Officials of CITES were responsible for legalising the open sale of poached ivory, often receiving healthy 'donations' for such auctions held in Burundi, Somalia and Singapore. Probably the most iniquitous legalisation by CITES took place in 1986 in Singapore when a stockpile of 270 tons of poached raw ivory was registered under the

Above: *The tusk of a young bull – he literally carries a price on his head.* Left: *A once magnificent pachyderm reduced to a bleeding carcass by ruthless poachers.*

CITES quota system. Overnight the Poon brothers, who then controlled one of the biggest poached ivory networks, became richer by US$7,5 million. According to the London *Observer* the grateful traffickers donated US$200 000 to the CITES secretariat.

When this scandalous collusion was uncovered it was the last straw for many conservationists who had previously supported the economic use of ivory and other elephant by-products to ensure the animals' long-term survival and benefit to local populations. Too much money was being made by too many people dealing in illicitly obtained ivory for the situation to continue. Craig van Note, vice-president of the US-based conservation consortium Monitor commented: 'The fact that ivory gets legitimised by governments does not make it any less poached.'

With mounting evidence of the corruption prevalent at all levels of the ivory trade and the indisputable loss of elephants throughout their range, the ban in ivory and ivory products was inevitable, justified and timely.

After the ivory ban came into effect the southern African bloc petulantly threatened to withdraw from CITES and tried in vain to have the decision reversed at the 1991 CITES meeting in Japan. The 1994 CITES meeting in Fort Lauderdale saw the South African proposal to resume trading in ivory dropped from the proceedings before the meeting. But there has been much lobbying in advance of the 1997 CITES meeting in Harare when the elephant/ivory debate will no doubt feature high on the agenda.

The aftermath of the poaching holocaust left scientists with a mountain of facts and figures showing the extent of the slaughter. In 1979 a ton of ivory required an average of 54 dead elephants, mainly mature bulls. By 1987 the same ton of ivory required an average of 113 dead elephants. With most of the big bulls shot out in many areas, more and more females were being killed. These losses did not include all the infants and young juveniles left behind to die of starvation. During the 1980s between 71 000 and 79 999 tons of ivory were sent out of Africa, representing about 700 000 dead elephants. This did not include indirect loss of the young or tuskless individuals killed in the melee of the slaughter. Over 80 per cent of the tonnage was illegal poached ivory.

In some areas where elephant populations were decimated by poachers the elephants are now breeding well and re-establishing themselves. In Tsavo, if all goes well, the elephant may once again change the regenerated *Commiphora* woodlands to a more open grassland regimen, bringing a natural cycle into motion once again. Sadly, however, the black rhino will no longer be part of this cycle.

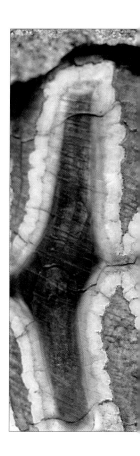

In other areas, however, the effect on the herds was far more dramatic and in cases of intensive poaching elephants stopped breeding because of harassment and the lack of any mature bulls capable of successful mating. In some areas the slaughter was so intense that not only the mature bulls were wiped out, but all tusk-bearing adults, matriarchs and adult breeding cows. All that remained were shell-shocked remnant populations or orphaned juveniles and sub-adults. How such remnant populations will proliferate and develop is a cause for concern, since the loss of two generations seriously impedes their future development. Without the guidance and teaching of the adults and the benefit of the breed herd's collective memory, which spans many generations, how will the young, inexperienced survivors know where to find food and water in times of drought, follow migration routes for seasonal feeding patterns and avoid contact and conflict with man? The presence of adults also gives the young the guidelines for social responsibility, hierarchy, group care of the young and in fact the whole complex fabric of elephant society. Only time will tell how and if these delinquent populations can survive to overcome these problems.

In certain areas such as Somalia, Sudan, Chad, Mauritania and Mozambique, the slaughter was so complete that there are not enough viable breeding animals left to re-establish the elephant population unless new specimens are introduced.

The elephants' long-term survival and recovery depends on the ivory ban remaining intact. Across Africa caches of weapons and ammunition lie hidden, stockpiles of ivory remain hoarded, smuggling routes lie dormant — all waiting for the day that a legal ivory trade may be resumed so the market can be flooded with poached ivory.

The culling controversy

Culling or population reduction exercises have been part of game management in Zimbabwe for a long time. Culling has been used to prevent numbers of certain species building up to levels — determined by parks researchers — where imbalances occur. One early example of a population reduction exercise carried out in Hwange was the systematic reduction of predators, principally lion, to enable most herbivores to increase from their low numbers at the time. Even the African wild dog, one of the world's most endangered predators, was shot on sight by parks staff until the early 1960s.

Undoubtedly the most publicised animal to have been culled on a regular basis is the elephant. Levels of population reduction have been based on population densities considered optimal for the sustainable utilisation of Hwange's woody vegetation. Hwange's last elephant cull was in 1988 and now the park's estimated population is far in excess of what is considered to be optimum. Elephant pressure on fragile areas such as Sinamatella is all too evident. Limited, regular culling could quickly depopulate the area of most of its resident population by encouraging emigration and dispersion. This would give the vegetation a respite, provided impala are culled intensively as well. (The area's herbivore biomass indicates that impala are having an even greater impact than the elephant.)

The Zimbabwean authorities made the by-products of past culls available to the local rural populations. As culling primarily invol-

Below: *Details of the M6 molar tooth of a mature cow shot in a culling operation. The enamel and dentine show a distinctive pattern and wear.*

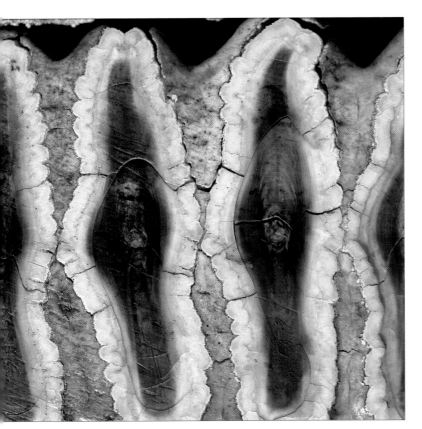

ves the elimination of entire family units, a large mass of cheap protein was provided to surrounding populations in the form of sun-dried meat. This action undoubtedly had good public relations value and improved the park's image in the eyes of the local people. They could no longer look upon national parks as areas set aside for 'wild meat' and elite tourists, and of no value to themselves or the country.

The hide of a culled elephant was cut into panels and tanned to be made into various leather goods, and even the bones were occasionally used. The ivory was retained by the state, and this is where conflict arises between the pro and anti ivory trade camps. Controlled auctions of registered ivory to licensed dealers were regularly held in Harare. The theory was that poached ivory could not get into the market if this legally obtained ivory was freely bought and sold, and the funds raised could be ploughed back into the system. However, there still seems to be much room for corruption. The Environmental Investigation Agency, a London-based animal and ecosystems rights investigation group, has established that there is a thriving illegal ivory trade in the subcontinent. South Africa appears to be the ringleader in this, but Zimbabwean business-men and officials are also involved.

The Environmental Investigation Agency produced a report that detailed several individuals' involvement in this insidious trade and the report mentioned a high-ranking officer within Zimbabwe's Department of National Parks. Elephants are not the only casualties in this trade. Members of the Department of National Parks, Zimbabwe Republic Police and Zimbabwe National Army have lost their lives in fights with poachers, in ambushes and during the course of investigations into the illegal trade.

The irony of the present setup is that none of the money raised at the official ivory auctions has been ploughed back into the Department of National Parks. The money disappeared into the maw of an insatiable central government Treasury and conservation has always received an annual pittance in the budget. In 1993 the budget for Hwange ran out some five months before the end of the financial year and all management, anti-poaching and patrolling activities quickly

ground to a halt. This gave the poachers free rein to attack the remaining rhinos, until the Department of National Parks received an aid grant of US$250 000 solely to reinstate anti-poaching activities. The warden then had to seek funds locally in order to establish the season's water provision programme to ensure money was available to pump essential life-giving water into the pans to maintain the park's viability.

Today the need to cull is becoming more and more debatable on the local scene. Worries grow that population census techniques are not accurate and the number of elephants has been overestimated. Computer-projected population figures rely on limited aerial transects without adequate confirmation of the elephants' status on the ground. Such population statistics came under heavy fire at the 1989 CITES conference in Lausanne. Dr Rowan Martin, Deputy Director of Zimbabwe's Department of National Parks and Wildlife Management, presented a computer-projected population figure for the African elephant of around 1,3 million with an annual decline of 1,8 per cent. This was vigorously contested by a legion of elephant scientists from around Africa and a figure of 600 000 to 650 000 is now more readily accepted.

Above: *A young bull poses, using a termite mound to gain added height and make his threat posture more intimidating. Unfortunately, this stance is ineffective in the face of a gun.*
Left: *Locals from Dete village pile into the carcass of a bull elephant after a culling operation.*
Right: *The skeleton of an elephant, killed as part of a culling operation. The brain cavity has been exposed, showing how deeply embedded it is in the surrounding honey-comb mass.*

and above all a lot of money, but it proved that countries such as Zimbabwe and Botswana could export their excess elephants to countries with depleted elephant populations.

The question of culling is not unique to Zimbabwe, but certain instances in other parts of Africa question culling as the final solution. In Lake Manyara National Park in Tanzania, which had one of the highest elephant densities, concern was voiced on the over-utilisation of the park's acacia forest and culling was considered, but did not come about. The elephants solved the problem themselves — they just stopped feeding on the acacia and the forest quickly regenerated.

Culling to maintain a static vegetation balance is, in essence, trying to maintain time in a capsule — a most unnatural state of affairs. Elephants quickly respond to factors reducing their population. After natural reductions in population, such as drought, elephants react by breeding at an earlier age and at shorter intervals. Man-made reductions in populations, such as culling, stimulate the elephants' biological response and put pressure on a sustained culling programme — the more you cull, the more you need to continue culling to maintain a static population level. The inherent danger in this method is an alteration to a sound genetic pool necessary for the species' future wellbeing.

The dramatic increase in Hwange's elephant population has not come about by reproduction alone. Increased human pressure in surrounding areas has driven elephants into the park, and so have the upheavals in Namibia, Angola and Zambia. As peace and stability return to the region, it is hoped that the elephants will go back to their home ranges in safety.

The elephant is the world's largest land mammal, but remarkably little is known of its population dynamics and demographics, social interactions, breeding biology, hierarchy and communication. Only in the last 15 years have we learned of the elephants' ability to communicate by infrasound over long distances. Also the occurrence of musth in the African elephant, though recognised in its Asiatic cousin for centuries, is only just being unravelled as an integral part in the mature male's breeding biology.

Only with long-term research of stable,

The present respite in culling operations in Hwange has allowed the population to grow and elephants are easily seen by most visitors, especially in the dry season. A proposed cull of 5 000 in September 1992 was called off owing to lack of funds in the department. The government pleaded for an international aid package for the 1993 cull, but nothing was forthcoming from the international community. No culls have taken place since 1988.

Zimbabwe has been involved in an exciting alternative to culling. The debilitating drought of 1991-92 crippled the country's south-east lowveld region, and in particular the Gona Re Zhou National Park on the Mozambique border. Clem Coetzee, renowned conservationist and former head of the Department of National Parks Management Unit based at Umtshibi in Hwange, proved the experts wrong by successfully capturing and translocating adult elephants. This required meticulous planning, skilled manpower unharassed populations will we ever gain a true insight into the elephant and its ability to live in harmony with its environment.

What does the future hold?

Worldwide attitudes to trade in wildlife, especially in endangered species, have altered drastically in the last decade. Movements such as Beauty Without Cruelty have launched massive public awareness programmes to alert an uninformed public to many of mankind's acts of cruelty to the other inhabitants of the planet. The demand for expensive sealskin coats plummeted when people found out that the coats came from infant seals and the most cost-effective way of collecting the pelts was for the hunters to club their brains out. A leopardskin coat loses its allure when it is realised that 18 leopards die to make one coat. Public outcry stopped many nations from hunting the great whales to near-extinction for oils, cosmetics and petfood. The deliberate netting and drowning of hundreds of thousands of western Pacific dolphins to catch tuna was met with massive consumer resistance. More and more people are coming to realise that wild creatures are not there solely to be exploited by man.

With this change in public attitudes, the future of the elephant seems brighter than in the past couple of decades. Without the pressure of the ivory trade populations have a chance to recover and to reclaim many areas of their former range. Obviously, as Africa's human population grows — in places at alarming rates — elephants will lose out on some of their range in the face of human expansion. It is the responsibility of Africa's governments to formulate cohesive policies that guarantee the future of national parks not as sacrosanct areas, but places to be used for the benefit of their country's people, economies and future generations. As populations grow, more land will be required to feed more mouths and these new areas required must be used wisely. Governments must realise that land is not finite and when one area is wasted it is highly irresponsible to move onto a new area to ruin. Even a continent the size of Africa cannot sustain such abuse.

Africa is losing viable habitat at an alarming rate. The Sahara advances at the rate of nearly 2 km a year due to traditional and now inappropriate land use; the Kalahari and Karoo drylands extend further each year, again because of bad land use. Hundreds of square kilometres of tropical rain forest disappear each month in uncontrolled exploitation. A sound long-term land use policy for all of Africa is urgently required, not only to preserve areas of wilderness to ensure the future of the elephant and Africa's incredible richness of wildlife, but also to safeguard the future of a healthy, well fed human population.

As elephant populations recover around Africa and as they become more confined to

Left: *A lone bull reflected in the water of a pan — a symbol of hope for a peaceful future for Hwange's elephants.*
Above left: *A large elephant herd moves across Dete Vlei – everything must be done to ensure that the magnificent herds of Hwange survive into the next century.*
Above: *Young elephants revel in play — here a young calf pauses during a playful session to relieve an itch after a glorious mud wallow.*

limited areas of protection and sanctuary, their management will become a prominent issue once again. Undoubtedly culling will become a necessary solution in areas where the park's size or lack of variation of the vegetation places a strain on the habitat. But the elephant is capable of regulating its breeding rates and as more information is gathered on the elephant's life cycle, the gun need not be the only measure we have to fall back on.

The elephant is part of the African scene, having evolved over millions of years. With thought and care it can remain a part of the African landscape for generations to come and provide aesthetic enjoyment and economic benefits to all.

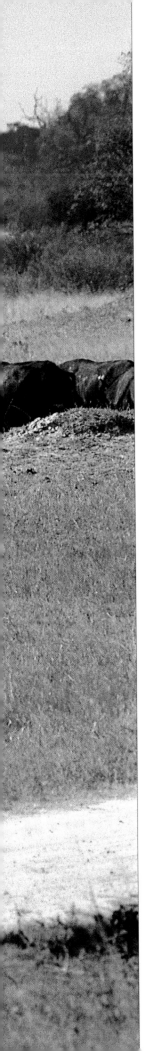

HWANGE'S FACILITIES

'The wonder of the world, the beauty and the power,
the shapes of things, their colours, lights and shades;
these I saw. Look ye also whilst life lasts.'

Inscription on a Cumberland gravestone

The visitor to Hwange has a wide choice of accommodation since there is something to suit everyone's taste and budget. Facilities range from basic campsites to luxury exclusive safari camps. Visitors can thus choose whether to plan a self-catering and self-driving trip, or to be based at a hotel or private camp and be chauffeured by experienced guides in the ubiquitous zebra buses or open four-wheel-drive vehicles.

The public camps

The accommodation offered by the Department of National Parks is excellent, well maintained and very inexpensive. The three primary camps are all situated in the park, but are close to the boundaries on account of the peripheral development policy. The largest of the camps, situated a short distance off the main tar road between Bula-

Left: *Hwange offers the tourist many opportunities for watching, studying and photographing big game.* Above: *A group of tourists in an open safari vehicle experience the magic of an African sunset while listening to lions roaring to proclaim their territory.* PHOTO: STEPHANIE GREAVES

wayo and Victoria Falls, is Main Camp. It caters for campers and caravanners, providing ablution blocks with baths, showers and toilets and braai (or barbecue) sites for cooking. The camp also has cottages and chalets with varying degrees of amenities and equipment, as well as fully equipped lodges. Electricity and running water are installed in all the units, though the visitor is advised to check what cooking and eating equipment is provided.

Visitors should also note that all mains electricity supply in Zimbabwe is 220 volts, which can create problems for those wanting to recharge VCR batteries, etc. Main Camp has other facilities to enhance the visit and a shop provides many basic foodstuffs. There is a curio shop for ethnic souvenirs, a petrol station and an excellent restaurant and bar — the popular Waterbuck's Head.

Sinamatella provides a similar range of

Above: *Viewing in vehicles with professional guides is one of the best ways to see and film game at close quarters.*
Above right: *Steam safaris offer steam and wildlife enthusiasts a combination growing in popularity.*

matella has a small kiosk supplying basic provisions, a curio shop, petrol station and, again, an excellent restaurant and bar called the Elephant and Dassie.

The third camp, Robins, is the most remote and smallest of the public accommodation facilities. The single or double chalets provide accommodation for up to 48 people, but again augmented by a well-maintained campsite. The most rustic of the camps, Robins provides open wood fires for all cooking; electricity is provided by a diesel generator with 'lights out' at 9 pm. The rooms have no running water, but ablution blocks provide all the basic facilities. Each room is equipped with a small paraffin fridge to help keep food and drinks cool — a godsend in October. Robins has a petrol station, a shop and bar, and the restaurant has recently reopened. Access is either from Main Camp and Sinamatella through the park, or by 80 km of dirt road from the main road at Matetsi.

Exclusive camps

In addition to the public accommodation at Main, Robins and Sinamatella camps, the parks department also offers exclusive accommodation at Nantwich and Deka camps near Robins, and Bumbusi and Lukosi camps near Sinamatella. These secluded and peaceful

Right: More luxurious accommodation is available at numerous safari camps in and around Hwange. Sikumi Tree Lodge provides a unique way of enjoying Hwange and its environs.

accommodation though the camp is considerably smaller, providing room for up to 70 visitors, not including campers and caravanners, at any one time. It is situated 45 km from Hwange town on the main Victoria Falls/ Bulawayo road, making access quick and easy, or it can be reached through the park from either of the other camps. Most of the rooms are self-contained with shower and toilet facilities and have mains electricity. Sina-

havens are for those who want to get away from the hurly-burly of life and they are fully equipped. Parks staff are on hand to assist with basic chores. Visitors must take all food and provisions required for the stay. Each of these exclusive camps caters for parties of up to 12 people, except for Nantwich, which can accommodate a party of 18.

Camping

As well as the exclusive camps mentioned above, the more adventurous can camp at some of the picnic sites at Kapul, Detema, Masuma, Shumba, Mandavu, Ngweshla, Kennedy 1 and Jambile. These sites are fenced in and provide toilets and borehole water, but the visitor must be fully self-contained. These sites are a must for those equipped and eager to fully enjoy and appreciate the tranquillity and serendipity of the African bush. A recent addition to the campsites are viewing platforms, such as those at Nyamandhlovu and Guvalala, where the public can book to stay overnight.

Private safaris

Several private safari operations have remote bush camps in the park where the visitor can enjoy the comfort of well-run and maintained camps, be wined and dined and yet enjoy the soul-stirring tranquillity of Hwange. Makololo and Linkwasha are two exclusive and remote private safari camps situated in the

wilderness area, deep within the park, where guided walks, drives by day or night, photography or complete relaxation are all on offer. Touch the Wild offers accommodation at the unique Sikumi Tree Lodge, the luxurious Kahatshana Lodge, the small and intimate Konondo Bush Camp and the sumptuous Sable Valley Lodge. Queen Elizabeth II and Prince Philip once stayed at Sable Valley.

Numerous other safari outfitters have a further choice of camps on offer close to Hwange's boundaries. Two camps recommended for easy access and quality of service are Ivory Trails, overlooking its own pan and close to Main Camp, and Jijima Camp, which nestles on the edge of a picturesque vlei and has direct access to the park at the Kennedy 1 vlei. An exciting overland trip is offered by Wild Horizons, starting at their Imbabala camp and ending at Jijima. This trip starts on a beautiful stretch of the Zambezi, allows visitors to travel for several days in an open vehicle through Kazuma, Matetsi and Hwange, camping under canvas, and finishes at JiJima.

Hwange Safari Lodge

The Hwange Safari Lodge offers luxurious, international standard accommodation. Situated close to the Hwange airport, the hotel is serviced by daily triangular flights between Harare, Kariba and Victoria Falls, allowing Hwange to be easily included in the itinerary of foreign tourists with limited time. Special packages, called Flame Lily Tours and run by Air Zimbabwe, allow travellers to visit most of Zimbabwe's tourist attractions at an affordable price.

Precautions

Visitors are wise to take precautions in all the rest sites and camps for wild animals have right of way and will exercise that right. It is advisable to carry a torch at all times when it is dark as some animals actually use human habitation as protection from predators. Main Camp has a daily ritual of several dozen wildebeest trooping onto the lawns around the lodges and spending the night there, to avoid being hunted by lion. This does not always work; several years ago the fuel station went unmanned for a day as the resident lion pride tucked into a wildebeest killed right up against the diesel pump. Hyenas prowl all the camps in the park and anyone unwise enough to leave anything that smells remotely edible lying around will soon lose it to the hyenas. This even includes pots and pans. The hyenas at Robins are particularly destructive and campers in all camps have to sleep under canvas to avoid the possibility of a messy amputation!

A family of ratels or honey badgers are particular favourites with visitors to Sinamatella. These pugnacious relatives of the mongoose are totally fearless and accustomed to the human presence. Their arrival in camp is signalled by the crash of displaced dustbin lids just after dark as the day's collection of debris

CENTRAL RESERVATIONS OFFICE
Department of National Parks,
P O Box CY 140, Causeway,
Harare, Zimbabwe.
Tel: (14) 70 6077/8
Fax: (14) 72 6089

REGIONAL BOOKING OFFICE
Department of National Parks,
P O Box 2283, Bulawayo, Zimbabwe.
Tel: (19) 6 3646
or 6 1018

AIR ZIMBABWE
Flame Lily Tours, Air Zimbabwe
booking offices in many countries in
Europe, North America and Australia
as well as most centres in Zimbabwe.
Harare: Tel: (14) 79 4481
Bulawayo: Tel: (19) 7 2051

HWANGE SAFARI LODGE
Private Bag DT 5792, Dete,
Zimbabwe. Telex: 51602 ZW,
Fax: (118) 337, Tel: (118) 331/2

TOUCH THE WILD
(Sikumi Tree Lodge, Sable Valley and
Konondo and Kahatshana camps),
Private Bag DT 5779, Dete,

Zimbabwe.
Telex: 5 1604 ZW,
Tel: (118) 356 or 273
or

TOUCH THE WILD RESERVATIONS
Private Bag 6, Hillside, Bulawayo,
Zimbabwe. Telex: 33492 ZW,
Fax: (19) 4 4696,
Tel: (19) 7 4589 or 4 1225

WILD HORIZONS
(Jijima and Imbalala safari camps),
P O Box 159, Victoria Falls,
Zimbabwe. Telex: 51685 ZW,
Tel: (113) 2004 or 2025
Fax: (113) 4349

IVORY SAFARIS
P O Box 55, Dete, Zimbabwe.
Tel: (118) 224

SHAMWARI SAFARIS
P O Box 53, Dete, Zimbabwe.
Tel: (118) 248

JABULISA SAFARI LODGE
P O Box 23, Gwayi, Zimbabwe.
Tel: (118) 2306

**HERTZ RENT-A-CAR AND UNITED
TOURING COMPANY (UTC)**
c/o Hwange Safari Lodge, Private Bag
DT 5792, Dete, Zimbabwe.
Telex: 51606 UCTWIKM ZW
Tel: (118) 393
or
P O Box 2914, Harare, Zimbabwe.
Telex: 22173 ZW, Fax: (14) 7 9294,
Tel: (14) 79 3701

LINKWASHA SAFARIS
c/o Sunshine Tours, P O Box 447,
Bulawayo, Zimbabwe. Telex: 33304
ZW, Fax: (19) 7 4832,
Tel: (19) 6 7791

GWAAI RIVER HOTEL
P O Box 9, Gwayi, Zimbabwe.
Tel: (118) 355,
Fax: (118) 268

ZIMBABWE SUN HOTELS
Central Reservations, P O Box
CY 1211, Causeway, Harare,
Zimbabwe.
Telex: 26340 ZW,
Fax: (14) 75 0133,
Tel: (14) 73 6644
or 70 7759

---

is picked through for tasty titbits. If kitchen doors are unwisely left ajar, the honey badgers will brazenly check out the kitchen and dining room for edibles and if the evening meal is unattended you can kiss it goodbye. The honey badgers regularly visit the restaurant and bar on their nightly rounds and are allowed right of way. Never, ever corner, threaten or harass a honey badger because you will come off worse. The honey badger is a vicious and tenacious fighter and even lions keep a respectful distance from them.

The grounds of the Hwange Safari Lodge have many large mature camelthorns (*Acacia erioloba*), which bear large, nutritious seed pods, and the elephants' collective memory has passed this information down from generation to generation. Human presence usually keeps females and young well clear, but to

Above: *The reception rondavel at the prestigious Sable Valley Camp.*
Left: *A professional safari guide and his apprentice show overseas visitors a mineral salt lick and advise on its importance to the wildlife.*

nonchalant males the grounds are no threat. After a gourmet evening meal, the visitor out for an evening stroll to help digestion and to watch the activity at the floodlit pan which the hotel overlooks, would be well advised to check which shadows move and which are stationary. Human night vision is particularly poor and it is amazing how difficult elephants are to see at night. Each camelthorn season — May and June — several visitors have close calls with elephants. More often than not the elephants warn people with a shake of the head and clatter of ears, to prevent people walking right into them. Sometimes, when both parties are taken by surprise, a mock charge will result. This is not a pleasant experience and causes havoc with the digestion! The simple rules are: don't get too close, don't push your luck and don't take chances.

Use common sense and stay in the lit areas, away from the trees.

The world's largest land mammal is normally a benign creature and poses far less of a threat than other, smaller inhabitants of the Hwange bush. Snakes and scorpions are common, though seldom seen, and some insects pack a mighty wallop so anti-histamine creams are well worth packing to relieve itchy bites and stings. Malaria is an endemic fever borne by mosquitos which are found everywhere in the wet season, but visitors are strongly advised to take malaria prophylactics all year round — better safe than sorry!

Bookings for all National Parks accommodation open six months in advance and visitors are advised to plan and book well in advance. Pitching up and hoping for the best can lead to disappointment, especially in peak seasons and

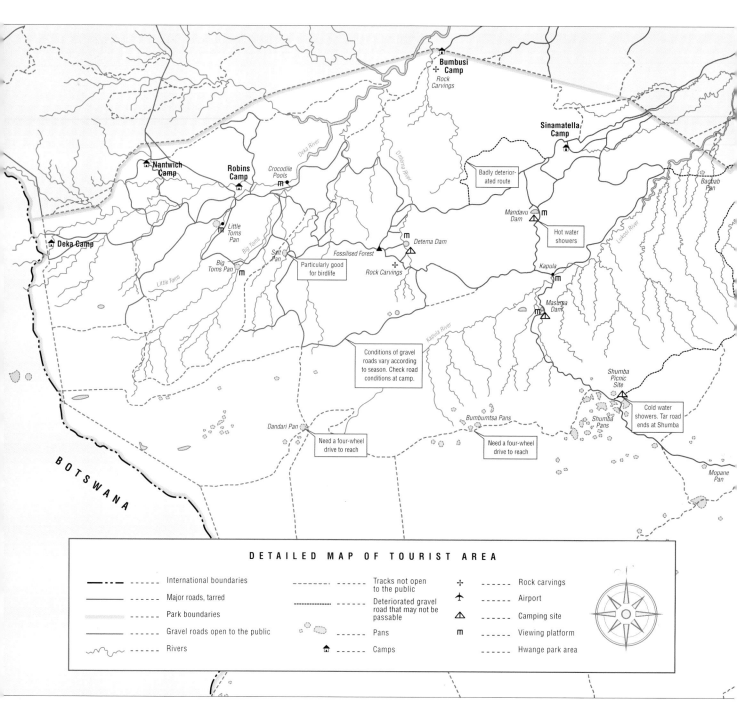

DETAILED MAP OF TOURIST AREA

International boundaries	Tracks not open to the public
Major roads, tarred	Deteriorated gravel road that may not be passable
Park boundaries	Pans
Gravel roads open to the public	Camps
Rivers	Rock carvings
	Airport
	Camping site
	Viewing platform
	Hwange park area

Map labels: Bumbusi Camp, Rock Carvings, Sinamatella Camp, Badly deteriorated route, Nantwich Camp, Robins Camp, Crocodile Pools, Deka River, Mandavu Dam, Hot water showers, Baobab Pan, Little Toms Pan, Deka Camp, Detema Dam, Kapula, Big Toms, Salt Pan, Fossilised Forest, Rock Carvings, Particularly good for birdlife, Masuma Dam, Little Toms, Big Toms Pan, Likosi River, Kapula River, Shumba Picnic Site, Cold water showers. Tar road ends at Shumba, Conditions of gravel roads vary according to season. Check road conditions at camp., Dandari Pan, Bumbumtsa Pans, Shumba Pans, Need a four-wheel drive to reach, Need a four-wheel drive to reach, Mopane Pan, BOTSWANA

school holidays. If the visitor would like to hire a car, this should be booked well in advance as vehicles are few and demand is high. Hiking is not allowed in the park and motorbikes are also not allowed so backpackers must rely on lifts from good-natured drivers or the services of Shamwari Safaris, which specialise in day trips into the park and overnight at picnic sites, when available.

Hwange has something to offer everyone's taste and expectations, be it total independence or lavish luxury, so that the visitor can make the most of the wild.

Watering points in the park

Many of Hwange's watering points are beyond the access of the average tourist and many require a sturdy four-wheel-drive vehicle to get there. The list on the following pages aims to help you gain maximum enjoyment from your stay in Hwange by highlighting a few of the waterholes that offer excellent game viewing opportunities, are easy to visit, offer a variety of attractions and have facilities for camping or for just viewing game.

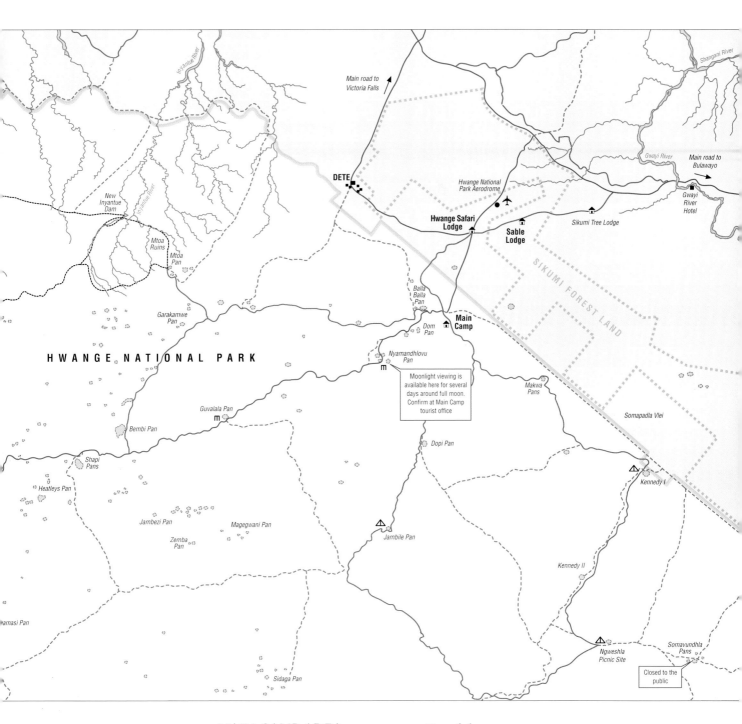

MAIN CAMP AREA

Nyamandhlovu Pan:

A large viewing platform and ablution facilities make this one of Main Camp's most popular (sometimes too popular) viewing areas. Easy access. Incredible concentrations of big game in the dry season. The highest density of giraffe in Africa. Excellent birdwatching in the wet season. Good for viewing all day long. Full-moon viewing can be booked at Main Camp, though the numbers are limited for this popular attraction.

Guvalala:

A smaller pan. Particularly good for afternoon viewing of large bull elephants. Viewing platform and ablution facilities.

Kennedy 1:

Picnic site. Can be booked overnight. High concentration of big game in the dry season.

Ngweshla:

Picnic site. Overnight booking. Good game year round, especially lion, elephant, buffalo, sable and roan.

Below left: *A guide tells Dutch visitors about the intricacies of the termite colony and its inhabitants.* Below right: *Discussing the morning's game drive before breakfast at Makololo Camp.* Right: *Robins Camp is the quietest and most rustic of the public accommodation facilities in the park.*

Jambile:
Picnic site. Overnight booking. Quiet, probably due to lack of salts in borehole water.

Mopani:
Alongside main tar road to Sinamatella. Good viewing in the dry season.

Shumba:
Picnic site. Overnight booking. Large, open area particularly good for antelope such as sable, roan and tsessebe. Large area flooded in good rains. Incredible concentration of birdlife when flooded.

SINAMATELLA AREA

Mandavu Dam:
Largest body of water in Hwange. Picnic site. Overnight camping. Good year-round for animals and birdlife.

Masuma Pan:
Viewing platform with ablutions on hilltop overlooking pan. Overnight booking. Good dry season game-viewing.

Kapula:
Small viewing platform with ablutions. Close to Masuma. Used to be excellent area for rhino.

Detema Dam:
Picnic site situated away from dam. Best in dry season. Good area for fossil trees.

ROBINS CAMP AREA

Little Toms:
Ground-level hide. Ablutions good bolt-hole when lions get too inquisitive.

Big Toms:
Viewing platform and ablutions. One of the best viewing areas in the park. Elephants drink within metres of the platform. Good for large predators.

Salt Pan:
Large shallow dam particularly good for birdlife, especially dry season. Several very large crocodiles do well here as the saline water attracts large numbers of animals. Good for lion and cheetah.

Crocodile Pools:

Crocodile-level viewing on the banks of the Deka River. Seasonal pools. Unusual for Hwange because of riverine vegetation. Good birdlife.

Several recommended pans such as Makololo, Somavundla, Kanondo and Imbeza are in safari concession areas and can only be visited if you stay with safari operators such as Touch the Wild and Linkwasha Safaris.

Many other pans can be found along the main routes between the various recommended pans and all of them are good places to sit, watch and wait and appreciate the wilderness as well as the animal and birdlife.

Larger mammals found in the park

Hedgehog	Whitetailed mongoose	Elephant	Impala
Chacma baboon	Banded mongoose	Dassie	Gemsbok
Vervet monkey	Selous mongoose	Black rhinoceros	Roan
Pangolin	Meller's mongoose	White rhinoceros	Sable
Bateared fox	Dwarf mongoose	Zebra	Tsessebe
Sidestriped jackal	Aardwolf	Warthog	Red hartebeest
Blackbacked jackal	Spotted hyena	Bushpig	Wildebeest
African wild dog	Brown hyena	Hippopotamus	Bushbuck
Striped polecat	Wildcat	Giraffe	Kudu
Honey badger	Serval	Grey duiker	Eland
Clawless otter	Caracal	Steenbok	Buffalo
Civet	Leopard	Sharpe's grysbok	Scrub hare
Largespotted genet	Lion	Klipspringer	Porcupine
Rustyspotted genet	Cheetah	Reedbuck	Bush squirrel
Slender mongoose	Aardvark	Waterbuck	Springhare

Left: *The end of the day at Makololo Pan, enjoyed by elephant and hippo alike.*
Right: *A grey heron stands silhouetted against the silvery waters of a salt pan, dwarfing a blackwinged stilt.*

Common bird species (resident and migratory)

Ostrich	Greenbacked heron	Ayre's hawk eagle	Dark chanting goshawk
Dabchick	Black heron	African hawk eagle	Gymnogene
Pinkbacked pelican	Dwarf bittern	Martial eagle	Cuckoo falcon
White pelican	Little bittern	Lizard buzzard	Osprey
Reed cormorant	Night heron	Brown snake eagle	Coqui francolin
Darter	Hamerkop	Blackbreasted snake eagle	Crested francolin
Grey heron	Marabou	Fish eagle	Redbilled francolin
Blackheaded heron	Openbill stork	Bateleur	Natal francolin
Goliath heron	Saddlebill stork	Augur buzzard	Swainson's francolin
Purple heron	Wood stork	Ovambo sparrowhawk	Crowned guineafowl
Great white egret	Woollynecked stork	Black sparrowhawk	Black crake
Little egret	Whitebellied stork	Little sparrowhawk	Purple gallinule
Yellowbilled egret	Black stork	Gabar goshawk	Glossy ibis
Cattle egret	White stork	African goshawk	African spoonbill
Squacco heron	Sacred ibis	Little banded goshawk	Greater flamingo

Above: *Part of a large herd of buffalo congregating at Nyamandhlovu Pan during the dry season.*

Lesser flamingo
Spurwing goose
Egyptian goose
Knobbilled duck
Redbilled teal
Cape teal
Hottentot teal
Whitefaced whistling duck
Fulvous/whistling duck
Redeyed pochard
Maccoa duck
Whitebacked duck
Secretary bird
Cape vulture
Whitebacked vulture
Lappetfaced vulture
Whiteheaded vulture
Hooded vulture
Peregrine falcon
Lanner falcon
Dickinson's kestrel
Yellowbilled kite
Blackshouldered kite
Bat hawk
Tawny eagle
Wahlberg's eagle
Booted eagle
Kori bustard
Redcrested korhaan
Blackbellied korhaan
African jacana
Lesser jacana
Painted snipe
Kittlitz's sandplover
Threebanded sandplover
Crowned plover
Blacksmith plover
Wattled plover
Little stint
Ruff
Common sandpiper
Green sandpiper
Marsh sandpiper
Greenshank
Wood sandpiper
Avocet
Stilt
Water dikkop
Spotted dikkop
Greyheaded gull
Whitewinged black tern
Spotted sandgrouse
Redeyed turtledove

Cape turtledove
Lesser gallinule
Moorhen
Lesser moorhen
Redknobbed coot
Crowned crane
Wattled crane
Grey lourie
Redchested cuckoo
Black cuckoo
Great spotted cuckoo
Striped cuckoo
Jacobin cuckoo
Klaas's cuckoo
Diederik cuckoo
Senegal coucal
Barn owl
Marsh owl
Scops owl
Whitefaced owl
Barred owl
Spotted eagle owl
Giant eagle owl
European nightjar
Rufouscheeked nightjar
Freckled nightjar
Mozambique nightjar
Pennantwinged nightjar
European swift
Whiterumped swift
Horus swift
Little swift
Palm swift
Redfaced mousebird
Narina trogon
Red kingfisher
Giant kingfisher
Greyhooded kingfisher
Brownhooded kingfisher
Malachite kingfisher
Wiretailed swallow
Pearlbreasted swallow
Greyrumped swallow
Mosque swallow
Redbreasted swallow
Greater striped swallow
Lesser striped swallow
House martin
European sand martin
African sand martin
Banded sand martin
Forktailed drongo
European golden oriole

African golden oriole
Blackheaded oriole
Black cuckoo shrike
Whitebreasted cuckoo
   shrike
Pied crow
Southern black tit
Grey penduline tit
Arrowmarked babbler
Laughing dove
Namaqua dove
Greenspotted dove
Green pigeon
Brownnecked parrot
Meyer's parrot
Striped kingfisher
European bee-eater
Carmine bee-eater
Whitefronted bee-eater
Little bee-eater
European roller
Lilacbreasted roller
Raquet-tailed roller
Purple roller
Broadbilled roller
Hoopoe
Redbilled hoopoe
Scimitarbilled hoopoe
Redbilled hornbill
Yellowbilled hornbill
Bradfield's hornbill
Ground hornbill
Blackcollared barbet
Pied barbet
Yellowfronted tinker
   barbet
Crested barbet
Greater honeyguide
Lesser honeyguide
Cardinal woodpecker
Bearded woodpecker
Rufousnaped lark
Fawncoloured lark
Sabota lark
Dusky lark
Flappet lark
Chestnutbacked finch lark
European swallow
Whitethroated swallow
Crombec
Barthroated apalis
Rattling cisticola
Tawnyflanked prinia

Spotted flycatcher
Tit-babbler
Marico flycatcher
Black flycatcher
Chinspot batis
Paradise flycatcher
African pied wagtail
Yellow wagtail
Richard's pipit
Lesser grey shrike
Fiscal shrike
Redbacked shrike
Boubou shrike
Crimsonbreasted shrike
Puffback shrike
Threestreaked tchagra
Blackcrowned tchagra
Pied babbler
Yellowbellied bulbul
Blackeyed bulbul
Kurrichane thrush
Groundscraper thrush
Capped wheatear
Familiar chat
Arnot's chat
Heuglin's robin
Whitebrowed scrub robin
Willow warbler
Yellowbellied gremomela
Redwinged starling
Yellowbilled oxpecker
Redbilled oxpecker
Marico sunbird
Whitebellied sunbird
Scarletchested sunbird
Yellow whiteeye
Buffalo weaver
Whitebrowed sparrow
   weaver
Greyheaded sparrow
Scalyfeathered finch
Spottedbacked weaver
Redbilled quelea
Cape widow
Whitewinged widow
Bronze mannikin
Jameson's firefinch
Blue waxbill
Blackcheeked waxbill
Pintailed whydah
Orangebreasted bush
   shrike
Greyheaded bush shrike

Longtailed shrike
White helmetshrike
Redbilled helmetshrike
Whitecrowned shrike
Boubou shrike
Wattled starling
Plumcoloured starling
Cape glossy starling
Blue-eared glossy starling
Longtailed starling
Black widow finch
Paradise whydah
Yelloweyed canary
Blackthroated canary
Streakyheaded seedeater
Blackeared seedeater
Rock bunting
Goldenbreasted bunting
House sparrow
Yellowthroated sparrow
Redheaded weaver
Masked weaver
Red bishop
Golden bishop
Cutthroat finch
Melba finch
Redbilled firefinch
Violeteared waxbill
Common waxbill
Shaft-tailed whydah

Right: Coqui francolins are common in the grasslands. They are smaller than redbilled francolins and have a more melodious call.

EPILOGUE

'The wilderness of only half a century ago, then so completely itself, has been reduced tree by tree, animal by animal, shadow by shadow, rock by rock, to its last rutted corners. The few remaining spaces have been infiltrated, divided up, domesticated, deprived of natural systems, denuded of natural processes, systematised, artificialised, sterilised, commercialised ...'

Peter Beard, *The End of the Game*

Over the years I have been visiting Hwange I spent many, many hours in the company of Stompie, a female white rhino, and her various calves. She was totally at ease in the presence of human beings and was probably one of the world's most photographed rhinos. Over time I developed a great affection for this lumbering, gentle matriarch. As rhino poaching escalated in recent years, it was always a relief to see her and her calf or to learn of her whereabouts from game guides. The last time I saw Stompie was in May 1993 when she was observed stealing a furtive drink in the dead of night at Dom Pan with her large calf and the large bull that her home range overlapped with. These normally placid creatures were furtive and literally running scared, their

---

Left: *An elephant bull peers through the dense teak and* Baphia *scrub typical of the Kalahari woodlands in the rainy season.* Above: *A lioness watches intently as a small group of buck move off to safer cover.*

tranquil world having been overturned by poachers. I was probably one of the last people to see Stompie, her calf and the territorial bull alive, apart from their murderers.

The following month the carcasses of Stompie and her calf were found by a National Parks patrol in thick scrub not far north of Dom Pan, the heart of her home range. They had at last fallen victim to the poachers. Vulture droppings were streaked across her sagging grey hide and a large part of the front of her face had been crudely chopped off by the poachers to obtain her unusual stunted horn. Her calf, whose horn was nearly as large as Stompie's, had suffered the same dreadful fate. The poachers would be a hundred dollars or so richer, but to the rhino horn barons of Lusaka and elsewhere, these horns were worth a small fortune. This was one more step in the complete and deliberate annihilation of a species.

For several months it was thought that Stompie and her calf were the last of Hwange's white rhinos, but extensive aerial survey eventually found two more, and it is hoped that one or two others may survive in the remote, dry western area of the park. Certainly the white rhino is no longer a viable, breeding species in Hwange — its chances of survival are slim. More black rhino remain in their last stronghold — the rugged, hilly country in the north of the park. It is estimated that there are presently about eight white rhino and about 40 black rhino in Hwange. The black rhino stronghold is an Intensive Protection Zone patrolled by parks staff and the army in the north of the park. Low numbers of rhino and the high chance of making contact with their defenders means that no poaching has occurred in Hwange since 1994.

With the rhino gone Hwange, Zimbabwe and the world are that much poorer. But we have the technology to save animals from extinction though they may no longer exist in the wild. Frozen semen, ova and foetuses provide a genetic hope for the future when either man's attitudes change or there is no longer a market for rhino by-products.

One encouraging move undertaken by CITES in September 1993 was the 'blackballing' of China and Taiwan because of their flagrant trafficking in illegal wildlife products, particularly rhino horn and tiger bones, both traditional Chinese remedies. The harshness of the wording surprised even the Environmental Investigation Agency as CITES has never before condemned individual countries for their internal usage of endangered wildlife products. This move is to be lauded as a first serious attempt to target the source of demand, the marketplace. The next target should be Yemen with its trade in rhino dagger handles.

In early September 1993 the Department of National Parks and Wildlife Management increased its tariff rates considerably and implemented a two-tier rate for local and foreign visitors. As the exchange rate of the Zimbabwe dollar is most favourable to regional and overseas visitors, national parks accommodation is still very good value for money, despite the big price hike. Even though a lower tariff is charged for Zimbabweans the parks have now been priced beyond the reach of the vast majority of Zimbabwe's population.

In recent national budgets the Zimbabwean

Right: *A zebra foal pauses at the roadside, seemingly unconcerned about the traffic on the road to Main Camp.*
Below: *A pair of magnificent sable bulls at Konondo Pan. Bulls often form small bachelor herds such as this.*

government once again slashed the fiscal vote for the Department of National Parks. The contempt with which the state seems to regard the nation's natural heritage defies all logic. In 1995 Hwange National Park earned over Z$30 million from direct tourism, not including revenues earned by private tour operators in and around Hwange, or trophy fees from controlled hunting in areas surrounding the park. Yet no funds are available for much-needed maintenance or repair work, especially to the road system.

Despite the lack of government support, Hwange's future looks reasonable for the near future, thanks to donor aid for keeping basic park functions operative. Certainly anti-poaching measures are essential and must be maintained for the foreseeable future. The recent financial injection came too late for the rhino, but there is hope for the elephant.

A final reflection seems timely. At long last plans have been approved by the government of Zimbabwe to allow the Department of National Parks and Wildlife Services to become a semi-independent body along the lines of a parastatal. This has followed an extensive and uncompromising political wrangle within the department's hierarchy, but it is hoped that now a definite path has been plotted for the nation's wildlife, and wilderness custodians can pick up the pieces and seek a common goal.

Now that the department can retain a percentage of its earnings, desperately needed funds will at last be available for road maintenance, upgrading tourist facilities and improving staff conditions and salaries. Above all, for Hwange this will mean the guarantee of a reliable and widespread supply of water during the dry season. The depressing sights of the 1994 and 1995 dry season, where boreholes and pans dried out and more and more animals were forced into smaller and smaller areas of the park, will hopefully be a thing of the past. No longer should 90 per cent of the elephant population utilise 10 per cent of the park and the inevitable over-utilisation of woody vegetation in these restricted areas be used as an excuse to promote culling.

In a recent report from the Minister of Environment and Tourism, elephant numbers in Matabeleland north (the area incorporating Hwange) were given as 19 400. In 1995, the

Wildlife Society of Zimbabwe undertook a 24-hour static count in near perfect conditions with a full moon and a bad rainfall season leaving limited surface water (hence virtually all possible water stations were covered) and counted 16 051 elephants in Hwange. This leaves a difference of 3 349, a number which could well be found in other wildlife areas in Matabeleland north, i.e. Matetsi, Kazuma and Zambezi National Park.

This is the first time official and 'amateur' census figures have closely corroborated since the late 1970s. This is a dramatic drop in a short space of time from previous figures of +/- 34 000 elephants in Hwange.

The 1995 elephant aerial census was co-ordinated with the Botswana census so that migrating elephants were not counted twice. The Hwange park census dropped to an estimated figure of around 24 000, a decline of 10 000 individuals. Hopefully this will lessen the clamour for further culling.

The Fort Lauderdale CITES meeting in November 1994 dropped the ivory issue from its agenda. Lobbying was far too intense and southern African countries trying to re-establish trading ivory failed to introduce a cohesive platform to embark on the ivory trail. The pro-ivory trade lobby will no doubt be better organised for the next CITES meeting in Harare in 1997. Friends of the African elephant will be hoping that their pleas will nevertheless fall on deaf ears so the elephant will receive a further reprieve.

In the heavily culled Kruger National Park in South Africa the killing has been halted for the first time in 29 years and the National Parks Board will not support regional attempts to lift the ivory ban at the 1997 CITES meeting in Harare. This is a healthy trend, especially as most of Kruger's elephants are refugees from Mozambique. The practicality of restocking Mozambique, Angola, Zambia and further afield with 'excess' elephants from Zimbabwe, Botswana, Namibia and South Africa is now real, though costly. But in terms of developing or re-establishing tourist industries and ensuring the elephant's existence into the 21st century and beyond, it seems a small price to pay.

The future of the elephants and Hwange is by no means ensured, but we can now look to the future with a great deal more optimism.

Above: *A pair of lions, probably brothers, work as a team in defending their pride and territory, thus increasing the chances of passing on their genes to the next generation.* PHOTO: DOUGLAS GREAVES

Glossary

ADAPTATION The process by which an organism becomes suited to its environment.

ANNUAL A plant that completes its life cycle from seedling to mature seed-bearing plant in one season and then dies.

BIOMASS The total weight of a species per unit of geographical area.

BROWSER An animal that eats mainly from the leaves, buds and twigs of trees and shrubs.

BUSH A general term applied to areas in southern Africa that still resemble their natural or original state.

CARNIVORE An animal that lives by eating the flesh of other animals.

CARRYING CAPACITY The number of animals of a given size which can be supported for a given time by the vegetation growing in that area without adversely affecting the vegetation production.

DEMOGRAPHICS The distribution of statistical information within a given population.

DIURNAL Term describing an animal that is active during the hours of daylight.

ECOLOGY The study of the relationship between living things and their environment, including both their non-living surroundings and other animals.

ECOSYSTEM The ecological system formed by the interaction of organisms and their environment.

ENDANGERED A term applied to an animal that is threatened with extinction, usually due to pressure from mankind either directly (from over-hunting to extinction) or indirectly (by changing the creature's habitat). The World Wide Fund for Nature's 'Red List' is a list of the animals most threatened with extinction.

EXTINCTION When a species no longer exists either in the wild or in captivity it is said to be extinct.

FAUNA The animal life of a locality or region.

FLORA The vegetation or plantlife of a locality or region.

GEMSBOK CUCUMBER The fruit of a creeping plant common in many dry areas. The fruit, though bitter, contains a lot of moisture and it is important to man and wildlife in the dry season.

GESTATION PERIOD The period of time required for a mammal to develop in its mother's womb from the date of conception, at mating, through to birth.

GRAZER An animal that feeds primarily on grass.

GREGARIOUS A sociable animal that lives in flocks or herds.

GUSU A vernacular term for areas of Kalahari sand.

HABITAT The immediate surroundings of a creature or plant which normally provides everything it requires to live.

HERBIVORE An animal that feeds on plants.

HERITAGE The natural environment left to us by our predecessors and which we are entrusted to hand on to future generations.

HIBERNATE A creature hibernates when it spends time in a deep sleep or torpor to avoid harsh climatic conditions such as cold winters.

HUNTER-GATHERER A term applied to nomadic tribes, such as the San or Bushmen of southern Africa who live off the land rather than relying on crops or livestock.

INCUBATION PERIOD The period of time required for a bird or reptile to develop in its egg from the time the egg is laid until the day it hatches.

INDIGENOUS An animal or plant that is native to the locality.

KOPPIE An Afrikaans name used throughout southern Africa to describe a small rocky hill or outcrop.

MAMMAL A term for the group of animals that are warm-blooded, have milk-producing glands, are partly covered in hair and bear their young alive.

MIGRATE Animals migrate when they undertake seasonal movements, often covering long distances, because of variations in food or water supplies due to changing seasons.

NOCTURNAL A creature that is active by night.

OMNIVORE A creature that eats both meat and vegetation.

PAN A natural waterhole.

PARASITE An organism living in or on another to its own advantage in terms of food and shelter.

PERENNIAL Persisting throughout the year, or for a number of years.

PREDATOR An animal that catches other animals for food.

PREY An animal caught by a predator.

RESOURCE Something available as a stock or reserve that can be used when required.

REPTILE A cold-blooded animal with a scaly skin, e.g. snakes and lizards.

SANCTUARY A safe place, such as a national park, where animals are usually free from persecution and threat.

SAVANNA Extensive areas of natural grassland.

SCAVENGER An animal that lives off the dead remains of other animals or plants.

SOLITARY A term describing an animal that lives alone without companions for most of the time.

SPECIES A term, singular or plural, for a group of animals or plants with common characteristics and which do not breed with others.

STILL-HUNTER A predator that utilises cover, camouflage and a short chase to catch its quarry unawares.

SYMBIOSIS The intimate living together of two kinds of organisms of differing species where such an association is of mutual advantage.

TERRITORY An area used by an animal for feeding and/or breeding, often defended against its own kind and sometimes against other species too.

THERMOREGULATION A mammal's ability to regulate its body temperature under different ambient temperatures.

TROPHIC LEVEL A term applied to a specific level or type of vegetation usually in terms of utilisation by herbivores.

VELD An Afrikaans term for bush.

VLEI An Afrikaans word used widely throughout southern Africa for an area of marshy ground.

WALLOW A mud or dust-bath in which animals lie or roll to cool off and obtain protection from skin parasites.

WATER TABLE The level below which the ground is saturated with water.

WEANING The stage at which a young animal is no longer dependent on its mother's milk and starts to eat the same food as the adult.

Bibliography

A Struggle for Survival — The Elephant Problem
Professor John Hanks
Struik 1979

An Outline of Geology in Rhodesia
J G Strydom
Government Printers 1978

The Penguin Atlas of African History
Colin McEvedy
Allen Lane 1980

Battle for the Elephants
Ian and Oria Douglas-Hamilton
Transworld Publishers 1992

Birds of Southern Africa
Kenneth Newman
Southern Book Publishers 1988

Elephants, Economics and Ivory
E B Barbier, J C Burgess, T M Swanson and D W Pearce
Earthscan Publications Ltd 1990

Elephant Memories
Cynthia Moss
Elm Tree Books 1988

Field Guide to the Snakes and Other Reptiles of Southern Africa

Bill Branch
Struik 1988

Kalahari — Life's Variety in Dune and Delta
Michael Main
Southern Book Publishers 1987

Landform and Landscape in Africa
J M Pritchard
Academic Books 1986

Mammals of the Southern African Subregion
J D Skinner and R H N Smithers
University of Pretoria
2nd Edition 1990

Painted Wolves — Wild Dogs of the Serengeti
Jonathan Scott
Hamish Hamilton 1991

Presidential Elephants of Zimbabwe
Alan Elliott
Delta Operations 1991

Rhino Road
Martin Booth
Constable and Company Limited 1992

Roberts' Birds of Southern Africa
G L MacLean

Trustees of the John Voelker Bird Book Fund 1985

Signs of the Wild
Clive Walker
Natural History Publications 1981

Spectrum Guide to Zimbabwe
Compiled by Camerapix Publishers Int. 1991

Southern African Spiders
Martin R Filmer
Baobab Books 1991

Survivors' Song
Delia and Mark Owens
HarperCollins Publishers 1992

The African Elephant — Last Days of Eden
B Norton
Swan Hill Press 1991

Trees of Southern Africa
Keith Coates-Palgrave
Struik 1988

Under Fire — Elephants in the Frontline
Environmental Investigation Agency 1992

Mammals of the Wankie National Park — Rhodesia
Viv Wilson
Trustees of the National

Museums 1975

Wankie — The Story of a Great Game Reserve
Ted Davidson
Regal Publishers 1977

Wankie Birds
Peter Steyn
Longman Zimbabwe 1974

Wild Places of Zimbabwe
Dick Pitman
Books of Zimbabwe 1980

Wild Flowers of Rhodesia
D C H Plowes and R B Drummond
Longman 1976

The End of the Game — The Last Word from Paradise
Peter H Beard
Collins 1977

The Roots of Heaven
Romain Gary
Michael Joseph 1958

Index